Christianity and Revolution

Christianity and Revolution

Tomás Borge's Theology of Life

Edited and translated by
ANDREW REDING

ORBIS BOOKS
Maryknoll, New York 10545

The Catholic Foreign Mission Society of America (Maryknoll) recruits and trains people for overseas missionary service. Through Orbis Books Maryknoll aims to foster the international dialogue that is essential to mission. The books published, however, reflect the opinions of their authors and are not meant to represent the official position of the society.

English translation © 1987 by Orbis Books, Maryknoll, NY 10545
Manufactured in the United States of America

Manuscript editor: William E. Jerman

Photo credit: MINT (Ministry of the Interior of Nicaragua), pp. 17, 21, 109, 134, 141, 151

Library of Congress Cataloging-in-Publication Data

Borge, Tomás, 1930-
 Christianity and revolution.

 1. Revolutions—Religious aspects—Christianity.
2. Liberation theology. 3. Nicaragua—Politics and
government—1979   . 4. Borge, Tomás, 1930–
I. Reding, Andrew. II. Title.
BT738.3.B67213 1987   277.285´082   86-23788
ISBN 0-88344-411-9 (pbk.)

My Personal Revenge

My personal revenge will be the right
of your children to school and to flowers;
My personal revenge will be to offer you
this florid song without fears;
My personal revenge will be to show you
the good there is in the eyes of my people,
always unyielding in combat
and most steadfast and generous in victory.

My personal revenge will be to say to you
good morning, without beggars in the streets,
when instead of jailing you I intend
you shake the sorrow from your eyes;
when you, practitioner of torture,
can no longer so much as lift your gaze,
my personal revenge will be to offer you
these hands you once maltreated
without being able to make them forsake tenderness.

And it was the people who hated you most
when the song was language of violence;
But the people today beneath its skin
of red and black has its heart uplifted.

LUIS ENRIQUE MEJÍA GODOY

Contents

Acknowledgments

The work that led to the publication of this book received wide support and encouragement from an informal network of persons and institutions spanning national and ecclesiastical divides in its affirmation of the gospel call for love rooted in social justice. I wish to express my thanks to those whose contributions have most directly facilitated my work:

• To the *compañeros* (intended in the fullness of meaning developed on p. 96, 102–3) of the Nicaraguan Baptist Convention and Baptist Theological Seminary who provided spiritual and logistical support: in particular to Dean Jerjes Ruiz, to Rector Roger Zavala, to American Baptist missioners Sheila and Steve Heneise, and to Southern Baptist Minister Douglass Sullivan, whose personal contribution in friendship and material support was, and is, invaluable.

• To Nicaraguan Baptist Convention director and FSLN National Assembly delegate Sixto Ulloa Doña for his assistance in circumventing bureaucratic bottlenecks and obstacles, and for personally introducing me to Tomás Borge.

• To Carol and Ping Ferry and to Episcopal priest Charles Demeré for their enthusiastic financial support of my overall work in Central America, as well as to former *Christianity & Crisis* editor Robert Hoyt and current *World Policy Journal* editor Sherle Schwenninger, whose editorial backing played a central role in the establishment of that work.

• To the Zeledón family of Estelí and the Torres Martín family of Managua for introducing me to Nicaragua.

• To Tomás Borge Martínez, to the martyrs of the revolution and the Nicaraguan people for reinforcing faith in an earthly incarnation of the kingdom of God.

• Finally, I thank the editors at Orbis for their enthusiastic backing of this project and for their helpful suggestions for improving the manuscript.

Introduction

A NEW KIND OF REVOLUTION

Only a few months earlier, his wife Yelba had been seized by the dreaded *Guardia Nacional,* personal army of Nicaraguan dictator Anastasio Somoza Debayle. She had been savagely raped, tortured, and killed, another of fifty thousand Nicaraguans sacrificed to the vanity of a tyrant as his loyal armed forces—organized and trained by the United States—turned their machine guns, tanks, and bombers on their own people. But on July 19, 1979, the Somoza dynasty was overthrown. Within a matter of days Tomás Borge Martínez, sole surviving founder of the victorious *Frente Sandinista de Liberación Nacional* (FSLN) and himself a victim of torture, confronted his wife's murderer as Nicaragua's new minister of the interior. "My revenge," Borge told the prisoner, "will be to pardon you."

Borge carried his personal forgiveness to his public office. When, in the tumultuous days following the collapse of the dictatorship, a lynch mob gathered outside the Red Cross building where National Guardsmen had found refuge, Borge hurried to the scene before the building could be overrun. "To what end did we carry out this revolution," he asked the crowd, "if we are going to repeat what they did?" The mob was stilled.

Such are the signs of the new order in Nicaragua, where a revolution that came to power through the violent overthrow of an even more violent dictatorship has made history by sparing the lives of mass executioners, torturers, and rapists, aiming—in Borge's words—"to eliminate the sin but save the sinners." Bibles, literacy teachers, and vocational instructors have been brought into the prisons to build a new life for former National Guardsmen. Those who have responded favorably have been transferred to unguarded

1

"open farms" where they take responsibility for their own governance in preparation for release. Hundreds have by now reentered society.

It is a revolution without parallel in recent history. In the political realm, a vanguard party organized along the Leninist model but inspired by the moral example of Augusto Sandino[1] has subjected itself to an open electoral contest with "bourgeois" opposition parties (held in November 1984), with the result that these now hold a little over a third of the seats in the National Constituent Assembly. In the economic realm, the Sandinistas have set up a system that combines capitalist and socialist characteristics in such a way as to give priority to production for satisfying basic human needs. And in the religious realm, the FSLN has integrated Christians and Marxists in one revolutionary movement, entrusting top government ministries to Catholic priests and lay persons.

It is this third dimension, this convergence of Marxism and Christianity, that is perhaps the most extraordinary development of the Nicaraguan revolution, a development in which Tomás Borge has played a critical role.

In 1969, a year after the Medellín Conference committed the Latin American Catholic Church to a "preferential option for the poor," Borge began approaching Nicaraguan Christians who were by then distinguishing themselves in their ministry with and for the poor. He sought out Father Ernesto Cardenal, founder of a Christian community in the Solentiname archipelago, and soon thereafter Franciscan Father Uriel Molina and Jesuit Father Fernando Cardenal, both of whom were working in Managua's lower-class Barrio Riguero.[2] At first the contacts were cautious and tentative, but they were to lead gradually to mutual trust and respect, and, finally, to collaborative resistance.

Today it can well be said that committed Christians play a larger role in the governance of revolutionary Nicaragua than they do in any other country. The Foreign Ministry is led by Father Miguel D'Escoto Brockmann of the Catholic Foreign Mission Society of America (more commonly known as Maryknoll); the Ministry of Education by Father Fernando Cardenal; the Ministry of Culture by Father Ernesto Cardenal. Edgard Parrales, formerly a parish priest in Managua, is now ambassador to the Organization of American States. Other prominent positions are held by committed

Catholic lay persons: Carlos Tünnermann serves as ambassador to the United States; Reinaldo Téfel as minister of social security and welfare; Miguel Vigil as minister of housing; Emilio Baltodano as comptroller general of the republic. The Christian presence extends into the National Constituent Assembly elected in November 1984 and charged with drafting the country's constitution. Four of twelve FSLN delegates named to the 22-member Constitutional Commission are prominent Christian laymen, including a top officer of the Nicaraguan Baptist Convention. Additional Christian representation is supplied by the Popular Social Christian Party (PPSC).

Working side by side, Christians and Marxists have amassed an impressive list of achievements in the first seven years of the revolution. The national literacy crusade headed by Fernando Cardenal has reduced illiteracy to less than a quarter of its former level. Medical consultations and vaccinations have tripled, and infant mortality has been reduced by more than a third. Land held in vast private plantations or ranches has been more than halved as land held by small farmers and farming cooperatives has more than quadrupled.[3] The government also has been generous in lending to small farmers, and when debts have threatened them (as they currently threaten family farmers in the U.S.A.), they have been absolved from payment. By favoring small farmers and cooperatives, the land reform has in turn shifted much of agriculture away from such export crops as coffee, sugar, bananas, and cacao toward such staples of domestic consumption as rice, beans, maize, poultry, and eggs. Food rationing (which may be supplemented by purchases on the open market) has also been implemented in order to ensure the basic nutritional requirements of life to all inhabitants. Despite the economic devastation being inflicted by the U.S.-backed counterrevolutionaries, or *contras,* a serious and sustained effort is being made to feed the hungry, heal the sick, clothe the naked, shelter the homeless, and rehabilitate the imprisoned.

THE RIGHT TO LIFE

It is against this background—a nation trying to reverse its history of destitution while being besieged by a U.S.-supported army—that a Sandinista *comandante* passionately confronts the "theology of death" with "the theology of life." His speeches and writings are laced with biblical references and allusions, from the story of Cain and Abel to the exodus, from the words of the prophets Isaiah, Amos, and Habakkuk to the gospel of Jesus and the letter of James. More importantly, as the reader will see from the selections in this volume, he demonstrates a practical grasp of Judeo-Christian theology only seldom attained by clerics and theologians (to say nothing of political leaders).

Tomás Borge challenges us to serious theological reflection by the power of both his moral vision and his moral practice. He insists that the right to life is our most important God-given right. While state-supported death squads do their grim reaping in the U.S. satellite states of El Salvador and Guatemala, and as capital punishment is reinstated in the United States, Borge's Ministry of the Interior has brought an end to that barbarous practice in Nicaragua. In fact, even life sentences are considered excessively cruel: the maximum prison sentence—seldom applied and frequently reduced—is thirty years.[4]

Torture has likewise been banned. Nicaragua recently became the thirtieth country to sign the United Nations Convention against Torture, which opens the doors of signatory nations to inspections by a body of experts. The only other Central American signatory is Costa Rica. The United States, which—with the exception of the Geneva Conventions—has yet to ratify any of the major international treaties regarding human rights, is not a signatory.[5]

Borge also reminds us that the right to life encompasses the right to the necessities of life, and that the requirements of the needy take precedence over the desires and property rights of the wealthy. He echoes Jesus' teaching that all nations are ultimately to be judged by whether they feed the hungry, clothe the naked, shelter the homeless, heal the sick. God is not interested in averages, but in evidence of compassion for those in greatest need.

A MORAL TRADITION

The key to understanding what has thus far distinguished the Nicaraguan revolution from other revolutions, particularly those involving profound social transformations, is to be found in the primacy given to moral concerns in the combination of Sandinism and Christianity that has guided its course. At the heart of both is a deep commitment to the sanctity of human life. Opposition to the death penalty originated with Augusto Sandino himself, who in the reactionary religious climate of the 1920s and 1930s developed a rudimentary theology of liberation of his own long before such a theology became a feature of the Latin American church.[6] His collected writings are a moving testament to the power of moral purpose in guiding his personal and political life. The example of Sandino is in turn repeated in the example of Carlos Fonseca Amador, whose intuition it was to resurrect the ideal of Sandino in the *Frente Sandinista de Liberación Nacional.*[7] Borge, writing from prison, recalls Fonseca's leadership in *Carlos, el amanecer dejó de ser una tentacion:*

> "If we allow ourselves to be guided by our personal feelings," he would say, "by anger, by the understandable impulse to repay our tormentors in the same currency, we will fall into the pattern of the sins we are fighting. If we wish to build a society made up of transformed human beings, mustn't we ourselves behave as transformed human beings? If we kill, if we commit abuses against a prisoner, in what way do we distinguish ourselves from our enemies?"[8]

Carlos Fonseca, like Sandino before him, was to be murdered by the National Guard.

Yet the moral vision of Sandino and Fonseca lives on in—among others—Tomás Borge, who has survived imprisonment and torture to take part in the revolutionary dawn. As minister of the interior he is today in charge of the police, the prisons, and state security. To counter the easy potential for abuse in these areas, Borge has made a critical distinction between what may be done in the course of defense against an armed adversary and what may be done once the adversary falls into one's hands. Captives, he insists, must be treated with the respect due any and all human beings, regardless of the enormity of the crimes they may have committed.[9] It is the sin, after all, and not the sinner, that is to be eliminated.

There is nothing accidental or coincidental about the biblical imagery that is so prominent in Borge's speeches and writings. Borge lists the Bible foremost among influences in his formation as a revolutionary, emphasizing that "the most basic influence on the development of a revolutionary is moral, not theoretical or ideological."[10] If this should seem surprising coming from one of the foremost socialist revolutionaries of our time, it is of a piece with the pattern of his life.

THE PATTERN OF A LIFE

Tomás Borge Martínez was born August 13, 1930, in the provincial city of Matagalpa, in the central mountains of Nicaragua. His father, a pharmacist, had served under General Benjamín Zeledón, resisting the U.S. marines who had intervened in the country's internal affairs in 1912. But it was his devoutly Catholic mother, Anita Martínez, who was to have the more profound parental influence. Through her he became involved in, and exposed to, conflicting elements of Catholicism. As an acolyte in the cathedral, he encountered the fire-and-brimstone teachings of Bishop Isidro Augusto Oviedo y Reyes; at home he was exposed to the life and works of St. Francis of Assisi, most notably through *The Little Flowers*. Finding the bishop's teachings on hell and eternal damnation to be irreconcilable with a God of justice, love, and mercy, he instinctively rejected the traditional Catholicism of the time while being deeply affected by the Christianity—"the true Christianity," as he insists—of St. Francis.

He also was deeply influenced by the westerns of German novelist Karl May. Although May had never visited the North American West, he used it as a setting for his high-minded characters, who exemplified honesty, loyalty, and bravery in defense of the poor. Borge repeatedly asserts that it was St. Francis and Karl May—not Karl Marx—who transformed him into a revolutionary.

At the age of thirteen Borge initiated his public opposition to the Somoza dictatorship by refusing to shake Anastasio Somoza García's hand when the latter made a visit to his secondary school. His nascent revolutionary sentiments soon brought him into association with Carlos Fonseca Amador. It was Fonseca who introduced him to the great Nicaraguan example of Augusto Sandino. Together they hunted for the bits and pieces of Sandino's written legacy that the dictatorship had sought to eradicate from national consciousness. Their search would lead to the formation of the *Frente Sandinista de Liberación Nacional.*

Despite his mother's wish that he study for the priesthood, Borge entered law school in 1951. According to classmate Carlos Tünnermann Bernheim (now ambassador to the United States), Tomás immediately distinguished himself as a natural leader and orator. So inflammatory were his speeches in denunciation of the dictatorship that on one occasion he had to go into hiding from the police. In 1956, just months before Borge was to graduate, the poet Rigoberto López Pérez assassinated Anastasio Somoza García, in what is commonly referred to as "the rendering of justice" for the murder of Sandino. Borge, whose university newspaper was printed on the small press of a friend of Rigoberto, was wrongfully fingered as an accomplice, and sentenced by a military tribunal to eight years in prison. In 1959 he managed to escape to Honduras; in 1961 in Nicaragua he banded together with Carlos Fonseca, Silvio Mayorga, Francisco Buitrago, Rigoberto Cruz ("Pablo Ubeda"), Modesto Duarte, José Benito Escobar, Jorge Navarro, Germán Pomares, Faustino Ruiz, and Col. Santos López of Sandino's original army in forming the FSLN.

When Borge began to initiate clandestine contacts with progressive priests in the late 1960s, he found himself face to face with a new kind of clergy, that had more in common with St. Francis than with the repressive clergy of his childhood memories. According to Ambassador Tünnermann, the person for whom Tomás claims to have the greatest affection is Father Fernando Cardenal. "When asked why, he [Borge] responds 'because it was Fernando Cardenal who recommended I read the Bible, and the Bible helped me enormously when I was a prisoner, helping me withstand the torture and the long years in jail.' "[11]

The Bible has since become Borge's favorite book, a prime source of material for his speeches. Crucifixes adorn one of his office walls in the Ministry of the Interior, and he frequently attends Mass in Father Uriel Molina's San Francisco de los Angeles church in Managua's Barrio Riguero, sharing communion and the embrace of peace with the urban poor and the mothers of "heroes and martyrs." It is an especially fitting place of worship, with painted murals recalling exemplary Christians in Central American history, from Fray Bartolomé de Las Casas and Fray Antonio Valdivieso, who in the sixteenth century boldly confronted the tyranny of the Spaniards over the indigenous inhabitants of the region, to Archbishop Oscar Arnulfo Romero, who just as boldly confronted the tyranny of modern elites in his native El Salvador.

A BROADER ETHIC

Borge is the first to admit that whatever claim he may have to being a Christian will not rest on symbolic manifestations of faith, but on the extent to which he is ultimately able to embody Christian virtues. As he confesses in his letter to Father Uriel Molina, he has not been altogether faithful to these in his personal life. Yet for all his human frailties and limitations, one may discern some personal qualities seldom seen in prominent public officials.

One such virtue is his honesty, which leads him to straightforward acknowledgment of abuses committed by government agencies under his supervision. One finds none of the lies, denials, "no comments," lapses of memory, and other evasions that have become the accepted standard for government officials. Instead one encounters confessions where they are appropriate, combined with a discernible will to correct transgressions. (Little wonder, then, that he has the confidence of numerous priests and ministers throughout Nicaragua, who know they can call on him anytime to resolve problems that come to their attention.)

Another quality is his mercy. "Let whomever is without sin cast the first stone." As noted earlier, Borge has boldly taken the lead in not casting the first stone, and in restraining others from doing so, even where the sinners are mass murderers, rapists, and torturers.

A third compelling virtue is Borge's humility, stemming from his profound admiration of St. Francis, and manifest in his address on the occasion of the anniversary of the death of Sandino (p. 50) and in his moving letter to Uriel Molina on the occasion of the latter's twenty-fifth anniversary in the priesthood (p. 133). Of particular interest is the way it informs his humaneness. Like St. Francis, he perceives that human beings are not the sole locus of value in the world, that the creation extends to the whole natural world, and that it has been pronounced good. It is well to recall that the words "human" and "humility" share a common root, most closely approximated by the related word "humus." From an etymological standpoint, to be *human* is to be an "earthling," just like the other beings with whom we share this planet. That is not to deny the differences among sentient beings, but to affirm that those differences no more justify treating other beings as mere things than do similarly arrogant sentiments of racism, sexism, and jingoistic nationalism. As Borge declared to an ecological gathering:

> We need to acknowledge human beings and nature alike as ends in themselves. We need to realize that nature is the inorganic body of humanity, that humanity and nature together constitute a single reality, and that the end of all of humankind's struggles consists in building unity between human beings and nature; in so arranging things that nature, which provides the base for human existence, becomes a material, scientific, artistic, and spiritual extension of humankind's organic body.[12]

It is an ethic that fortifies our humanity by extending the reach and substance of our love, and correspondingly shrinking the domain of callous exploitation.[13] There is a revolutionary generosity in this, a profound humility, that reaches out in fellowship to the entire community of creation, seeking the full liberation and communion prophesied by St. Paul (Rom. 8:19–22) and embodied in St. Francis.[14] Thus Tomás Borge can conclude, as he did in his 1982 address to the Seminar on Saving Lake Managua:

> We come from the dreams of all who love humanity because they love nature and love nature because they love humanity. We come from the dreams of Sandino, of Carlos Fonseca, and we know where we are going; we are going toward that society in which—like St. Francis—we will be able to say to the sun, "brother sun," to the moon, "sister moon," to the stars, "sister stars," and to human beings, "brother and sister."

ABOUT THE SELECTIONS

The selections to this volume have been chosen to provide a documentary cross section of Tomás Borge's contribution to the development and application of a Christian theology of liberation within the Nicaraguan revolution. Nine of the fifteen selections are explicitly addressed to religious audiences (in the case of the two letters, to priests). The remaining six are included for what they reveal about applications of "the theology of life" to Sandinista policy and practice. Three are directed to the new leaders and enforcers of the revolution: Sandinista party members, the Sandinista police, and legal professionals. Three more address themselves to the practical applications of human rights and their ecological correlates. The arrangement is chronological, so as to better relate each piece to its historical context, and to make it easier to perceive the evolution of Borge's thought and practice.

As an aid to the reader, the selections are introduced and annotated to supply historical context, identify biblical references, and fill in the gaps likely to confront the English-speaking public. Brief annotations are bracketed within the text; longer references are footnoted and listed at the end of each selection.

NOTES

1. Augusto Sandino led a guerrilla war of resistance against occupying U.S. Marines between 1927 and 1933, when the Marines were withdrawn. Though a brilliant military strategist and tactician, he is today becoming even better known for his farsighted moral and political thought, which encompassed elements of a theology of liberation and a detailed proposal for a Latin American confederation to counteract U.S. Monroe Doctrine pretensions in the hemisphere. Sandino was assassinated in 1934 on the orders of Anastasio Somoza García, founder of the Somoza dynasty. All attempts to recover his remains have been unsuccessful, prompting Tomás Borge to remark that he has arisen in the Nicaraguan people.

2. Significantly, it was in Nicaragua that Ernesto Cardenal risked the transition from cloistered monk to activist priest. Influenced by his mentor Thomas Merton, Father Cardenal became the catalyst who transformed poor fisherfolk and farmers on islands in Lake Cocibolca (also known as Lake Nicaragua) into the gifted theological community that created *The Gospel in Solentiname* (4 vols., Maryknoll, NY: Orbis Books, 1976–1982).

3. For an in-depth look at the story behind these statistics, see Thomas W. Walker, ed., *Nicaragua: The First Five Years* (New York: Praeger, 1985). It is interesting to note that in accord with the jubilee ethic (Lev. 25), land is

being handed out in a form of trusteeship rather than as a commodity. Recipients, who receive their land free of charge, may pass it on to their designated heirs, but may neither sell nor subdivide it, to prevent the joining of field to field and house to house decried by the prophet Isaiah.

4. The abolition of the death penalty, torture, and prison sentences of more than 30 years was established in Articles 5 and 6 of the Statute on the Rights and Guarantees of the Nicaraguan People issued on August 21, 1979. These provisions have now been incorporated in the draft constitution, whose Article 59 declares: "The right to life is inviolable and inherent to the human being. There is no death penalty in Nicaragua." Article 71 adds: "No one shall be subjected to torture or to any penalty or treatment that is cruel, inhuman, or degrading. No punishment may be imposed for more than 30 years." Borge's Ministry of the Interior has, in addition, refrained from the use of tear gas for "crowd control."

5. Nicaragua is also one of only 35 countries to have signed the Optional Protocol of the United Nations Covenant on Civil and Political Rights, empowering citizens who have exhausted domestic remedies for alleged violations to appeal to the United Nations Human Rights Committee. Costa Rica is the only other Central American signatory. Neither the United States nor any of the countries of the Soviet bloc has signed.

6. Giulio Girardi, "La Teosofía de la Liberación de Sandino," *Amanecer,* 32–33 (January-February 1985), pp. 30–35. For Sandino's opposition to the death penalty, see his Manifesto to the People of Nicaragua of October 6, 1927, in Sergio Ramírez, *Augusto Sandino: El Pensamiento Vivo* (Managua: Editorial Nueva Nicaragua, 1984).

7. Carlos Fonseca founded the FSLN with Tomás Borge and Silvio Mayorga in 1961. Though he was killed by the National Guard in 1976, he is today honored in Nicaragua as "Commander-in-Chief of the Revolution." An eternal flame lights his tomb on Managua's waterfront, in front of the ruins of the old cathedral.

8. Tomás Borge, *El Axioma de la Esperanza* (Bilbao: Desclée de Brouwer, 1984), p. 42.

9. See *Human Rights in Nicaragua: An Americas Watch Report* (July 1985), pp. 17–70, for an assessment of Nicaraguan performance in these areas.

10. For the full text of the interview, see "Tomás Borge Talks About the Revolution" (interview with Andrew Reding), *In These Times,* Sept. 18–24, 1985, pp. 16, 22.

11. Interview with Andrew Reding, Washington, D.C., January 31, 1985.

12. "El Xolotlán era un lago de singular belleza," in *Forjando una Política Ambiental* (Managua: IRENA, 1984), p. 60.

13. This ethic derives from Sandino himself, who forbade his soldiers to

hunt monkeys despite the fact that they are generally accepted as food in Central America. Questioned about this policy by a hungry officer, Sandino replied: "Don't you feel any remorse about killing beings similar to ourselves solely on account of not being able to stand a little hunger? . . . And don't you take into account the great service they render us by announcing the approach of the enemy with their furious screams? It is for all these reasons I don't want them killed, because they, the monkeys, are our good *compañeros.*" (Instituto de Estudio del Sandinismo, *El Sandinismo: Documentos Básicos* [Managua: Editorial Nueva Nicaragua, 1983], p. 202).

14. Such is the import of the Sabbath, sabbatical year, and jubilee legislation in the law of Moses, directing the faithful to respect the rights of all one's neighbors, including not only the poor and the alien, but domesticated and wild animals as well. It is an ethic later developed by Hosea in his prophecy of a new covenant with "the wild beasts, the birds of the air, and the things that creep on earth," where bow and sword and weapon of war shall be swept off the earth, "that all creatures may lie down without fear" (2:18).

1

Letter to Father Ernesto Cardenal
(1969)

This letter—written exactly a decade before the revolutionary triumph—marks an historic turning point for both the nascent revolutionary movement and the church, for it led to the first meeting between key figures of the Sandinista and progressive church movements in Nicaragua. Tomás Borge was then a clandestine guerrilla organizer; Ernesto Cardenal was liberating the artistic and theological creativity of agricultural and fishing communities on the islands of Solentiname in Lake Cocibolca.

With painful honesty, Borge explains how he rejected a Catholic Church—and the god it represented—characterized by its abandonment of the poor and the outcast. Though shocking from the standpoint of conservative religiosity, it is nevertheless a powerful affirmation of biblical faith. For in the light of Jesus' revelation of a loving God's preoccupation with the welfare of the poor and the oppressed, Borge is reaffirming the primacy of the First Commandment—the injunction against worshiping false gods— by pleading for a resurrection of genuine discipleship in the church.

Father Cardenal:

I am fulfilling a desire I've long had: to write you. I had originally been thinking of writing you a long and detailed letter. I changed my mind. I'd rather speak with you.

Owing to the circumstances in which I live, it is impossible for me to come to you in conformity with the courtesy and respect you deserve from me. It is you who will have to come to me. Speaking with you will be like receiving a long-awaited visit from a good friend.

We have renounced all the pleasures of life: we cannot even satisfy the elemental need to see the street and the incomparable spectacle of the coming and going of human beings. In a certain sense we are monks, with the difference that death is always stalking us. But we are happy.

I was educated in the Catholic faith, from whose beliefs I distanced myself with disgust.

I knew a God who joyfully rang the church bells and dressed up when General Somoza would visit León. A God who proudly received the candle offered by the calloused hand of a *campesino*, but refused to redeem him from his poverty, placing himself on the side of the landlord. A God who forgave the heavy sins of the rich, but forbade poor young women pregnant with "natural" child from entering the church.

For me this situation represented the incarnation of absolutism, and was responsible for my Manichaeism [against the institutional church], since overcome.

I slew that god without mercy within my conscience. It would seem, however, that God does not wish to die.

In the jungles of Colombia there has been a new Bethlehem. Camilo Torres told us so before dying, or perhaps told us so in dying. And he also told us there are mangers and Bethlehems in other places. Will the council be another Bethlehem?[1]

I have watched this new God take birth within me—I don't know why this reminds me of my mother—and I see how this God is growing. But it is not a spontaneous growth. It grows because it is being fed by the preaching of Father Juan Carlos Safaroni in Uruguay, and by the eulogy of Father [Ernesto] Cardenal upon the death of [Nicaraguan poet] Fernando Gordillo. To be sure, this God lives a precarious life within me. The more it grows, the more food it needs. Its vigorous development will depend on the immediate attitude of the church, or at least of its honest and progressive sector. Otherwise it will again die of starvation. If it dies, it will never again be revived. Father, I await you.

Tomás Borge

P.S.: My identity is unknown to the person carrying this letter.

NOTES

1. The Second Vatican Council concluded in late 1965, and was applied to Latin America at the Second General Conference of the Latin American Episcopal Council (CELAM), held in Medellín, Colombia, in August 1968. The Medellín Conference "preferential option for the poor" was prefigured by Colombian priest-sociologist Camilo Torres, who joined a guerrilla group and died in combat in February 1966 after peaceful efforts to achieve a measure of social justice proved fruitless.

2

The Police and Children
(1979)

Children play a special role in the Gospels. Jesus tells us we shall have to be as children to enter the kingdom of God, and reserves one of his direst warnings for those who would harm them. Herod, on the other hand, sees children as potential subversives, and orders them killed.

Children have played a similar role in the Nicaraguan revolution. Unable in their youthful innocence to accept the barbarities and corruption of Somoza's Nicaragua, they joined their adolescent brothers and sisters on the barricades in defense of their future. For like Herod, Somoza was a child-slayer. Not only did he consign children to the violence of disease and hunger, but once he began to feel threatened by them his National Guard began house-to-house searches, slaughtering the country's youth by the droves with scant regard for age. Managua's central park, the Parque Luis Alfonso Velásquez, *commemorates a 9-year-old Christian activist shot and then run over by the National Guard.*

This speech was presented to the First Gathering of Police and Children in Managua's Plaza de la Revolución *on December 8, 1979. In it Borge emphasizes the complete reversal in the relationship between police and children that has been brought about by the revolution and the creation of the Sandinista police.*

The early date of this speech needs to be kept in mind as Borge describes the appalling conditions children are living under, condi-

tions inherited from the Somoza dynasty. The figures have since improved dramatically, as reflected in the striking descent in infant mortality—from 12 to 7.5 percent—achieved by 1983. Also worth noting is the reference to the counterrevolutionary efforts already underway less than five months after the revolutionary triumph.

Borge with child held by mother

"Our children are the garden of the revolution."

Two thousand years ago a mother gave birth to a child who told us to love one another. That principle holds for Sandinista revolutionaries. Like the Christians, we proclaim the necessity of loving one another.

And when we call for love, we refer to the people. Love is in the heart of the people. When we castigate the enemies of the people, we do it out of love for the people. When we punish those who murdered the children, we do so out of love for our children, because loving one another does not mean letting Herod loose on the street. Loving one another means forcefully and energetically confronting the Herods who murdered our children.

And the new Herods as well, because those who oppose this revolution, who wish to obstruct this revolution, who seek to cast a dark cloud over the revolutionary dawn, those too are Herods, and we will not permit anyone to obstruct the future of the children of Nicaragua.

THE GARDEN OF OUR REVOLUTION

Children, do you know what gardeners do with flowers? They care for each flower. They water them every day. . . . You children are like flowers to the revolution. You are the garden of the revolution, and we the revolutionaries, the Sandinista police, the soldiers of our army, are the gardeners who are going to care for the flowers of our revolution throughout every single day.

Children, do you know what human beings do with their eyes? They take care of their eyes more than anything else. They protect them, because they are very sensitive. And you, children, are the eyes we take care of with so much love, so much affection, so much self-denial. Flowers, eyes, glowing suns; you children are the coddled ones, the beloved ones, for whom we are ready to give up the last drop of our blood.

It is not enough, however, to express love with words. It must be expressed with deeds, and we must therefore address ourselves to some frightening and painful statistics. Infant malnutrition in our country has risen to 70 percent: out of every hundred children, seventy are malnourished. Of every thousand children who are born, two hundred die. I think our primary task is to solve this problem of the health of our children, because at this very moment when you children of Nicaragua are so joyful here in the plaza, there are hundreds of thousands of children in the hospitals who lack adequate medical attention, who lack the medicines they need, and who are dying; and we cannot let these flowers die. We have to find a way to solve this extremely serious problem.

AN APPEAL TO THE WORLD

We therefore call upon the world, upon all the men and women of the world. Help us so our children won't die.

All healthy children, all healthy adults, have something to contribute to keep our children from dying. And to those who speak of human rights, to those who go pamphleteering about the streets saying that human rights are not respected in Nicaragua, we ask them to follow through on these human rights. Let them help us keep our children from dying, instead of going about uttering empty words.

Those who publish things saying they don't think the police should be called *Policía Sandinista*, would do better to help us instead of indulging in a lot of foolishness. With their money and resources, they could be helping us keep our children from dying. . . .

Children of Nicaragua, Sandinista children of Nicaragua, the *Policía Sandinista* is your friend. When you walk the street, you can be assured you will find in the policeperson a brother, a guide, a protector. When you go about the streets of the city, you can rest assured the Sandinista police will come to you with smiles on their faces and with hearts full of love for our children.

Our children are heroes of the revolution. You don't need to search for artificial cradles through marijuana and other drugs, which are harmful to children and adults. Today there is a drug stronger than all the others, the drug of the revolution, the only one our Sandinista children will imbibe.

It is time—because it is getting late even in the midst of this dawn of smiles and children—to go break open the *piñatas*, to go eat ice cream and sweets.[1] Children: the *piñatas*, the sweets, and the love of the Sandinistas await you in the rear of this plaza.

¡Patria Libre o Morir![2]

NOTES

1. *Piñatas* are hanging pots or boxes filled with sweets, which the children break open with sticks.

2. "A free homeland or death!," Sandino's famous refrain, reminiscent of Patrick Henry's "Give me liberty or give me death," itself reminiscent of the saying of Aeschylus (525–456 B.C.), "Death is better, a milder fate than tyranny."

3

Human Rights
and the Nicaraguan Revolution
(1980)

What follows is the transcript of Tomás Borge's October 10, 1980 presentation in Managua before a delegation sent by the Washington-based Inter-American Human Rights Commission to evaluate conditions in Nicaragua.

The presentation is remarkable in several ways. First, for the power of its honesty. Borge presents the dirty linen along with the clean, shares both dreams and frustrations, and finally asks his visitors for their assistance in turning Nicaragua into a showcase of respect for human rights.

Secondly, he provides us with an intimate but unromanticized view of the turbulent transition period following the revolutionary triumph in July 1979, showing us the irresponsibility, the looting, the urge for revenge, that accompanied the more heroic and noble manifestations of that period. Yet he does so sympathetically, helping us empathize with the feelings of a long-suffering people.

But to understand is not to condone, and rather than ride the tides of popular passion, Borge repeatedly challenges his hearers, using his personal authority to set moral examples that provide glimpses of a new world, of a new society founded on respect for human rights and characterized by generosity.

Perhaps I should begin by saying that in every country there are but two possibilities: either you side with human dignity and respect for human rights, or you oppose them. There is no other possibility. Leaving aside possible nuances, and without trying to fall into Manichaean positions, either we side with human rights or we oppose them.

The political leadership of this revolution and the government it has formed have made the firm and irreversible decision to side with human dignity, with human rights. We have obviously fallen short of perfection in practice, yet the most important thing is the strategic and historic decision to side with human dignity. That is why we invited you here.

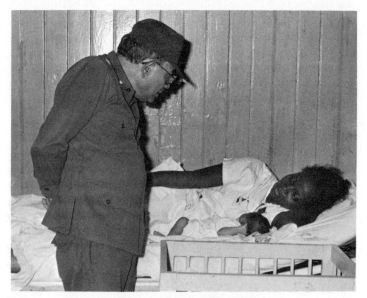

Borge with woman and baby

*"We would like to become a shining example of respect
for human rights."*

In speaking of human rights we must recall the tyranny of the Somoza dictatorship. For half a century Nicaraguans were placed before firing squads and subjected to torture chambers without so much as due process. Somoza's government specialized in violating all the laws, even within the juridical norms then prevailing in this country, which were different from today's because—with the revolution not yet having had time to change this obsolete legal structure—there is now incongruity between the laws of the past and the principles of our nascent revolution. But Somoza systematically violated his own government's legal framework.

NOTHING TO HIDE

The excesses of Somoza's tyranny are amply known to you, even though a criminal like Somoza does all he can to hide the truth. For us it has been a matter of principle not to try to hide anything, not even our mistakes, not even the abuses that have been committed. But naturally the Somoza tyranny did all it could to conceal the darkest aspects of the repression.

You were never informed about the peasants who had grease spread on their genitals so that the dogs would eat them, the men who were scalped alive with straight razors, and had salt and vinegar rubbed in to intensify their suffering until they died. Nor were you able to speak with the peasant women in the northern regions of the country, almost all of whom were raped. Nor are you likely to have been aware of the peasants who were buried alive in the mountains, or of the frightening number of victims: over one hundred thousand Nicaraguans were murdered.

If you can imagine it, there isn't a family in Nicaragua that hasn't been a victim of the repression—not even Somoza's own family. Edgar Lang, a Sandinista martyr and hero, was a relative of Somoza's, just as many other members of Somoza's family were victims of repression. Somoza's repression so stretched the limits of barbarism as to affect his own family as well as the families of his supporters. That there wasn't a single *somocista* family that was spared the effects of the repression should give you an idea of its magnitude.

RESENTMENT AND HATRED

Of course all this repression led to an enormous buildup of resentment in the Nicaraguan population, so that anyone thought to have had anything to do with the National Guard is hated. We have even tried to rescue some former National Guardsmen by putting them to work. In some cases the workers have tolerated them out of a sense of discipline, yet they've given them the cold shoulder, refusing to talk to them, making their lives miserable. The Guardsmen are not accepted, both for the reasons I've already mentioned and because they also stole from their victims. They were murderers, thieves, torturers, and rapists. That's what they were, and what they continue to be in the places to which they have fled.[1]

Perhaps the worst crime committed by Somoza and his son was not that of killing Nicaraguans or turning National Guardsmen into criminals, but that of turning *children* into criminals. Because when you refer to the children who are being detained, you must realize that those children were trained to gouge out the eyes of prisoners with a spoon; this was one of the techniques used by those children who were monstrously deformed by *somocismo*.

The revolution has made the political decision to rehabilitate these children instead of putting them on trial. Unfortunately, some of them have been placed in facilities for adults. While the revolution builds new facilities for them, they are being kept apart in a separate section of the Modelo facility. We will remove them from there as soon as we can provide them with suitable accommodations. But we cannot allow ourselves the luxury of setting them loose on the streets, for that would be to turn them into delinquents. Without employment, and with all the deformities imposed on them, these youngsters would become thieves and murderers, and would come right back to jail for their new crimes. That is why we wouldn't be doing them any favor by releasing them; why we're going to transfer them to another site to rehabilitate them.

REVOLUTIONARY HUMANISM

The revolution made the historic decision not to put anyone to death. In fact these bearings were laid out in the course of the war itself, well before victory. I don't know if the tape recording still exists of my appeal to the Guardsmen pinned down in the Matagalpa barracks—it was broadcast over our clandestine radio station. I asked them to surrender, telling them they had nothing to fear. The Guardsmen never believed us—never.

After having been brutally tortured as a prisoner, after having a hood placed over my head for nine months, after having been handcuffed for seven months, I remember that when we captured these torturers I told them: "The hour of my revenge has come: we will not do you even the slightest harm. You did not believe us beforehand; now you will believe us."

That is our philosophy, our way of being. But think for a moment what it means to have been in our country in those days. You, Mr. President [Thomas Farer, president of the University of New Mexico]—suppose they had murdered your wife, as they did mine; suppose they had brutally murdered a child or sibling of yours, or raped your wife, sister, or daughter; and that you then come to power. It could well be that you too would display the moral stature shown by the leaders of this revolution in not seeking revenge against those who had harmed them. But we cannot expect the same attitude from the great mass of combatants who saw their brothers, sisters, and children fall; whose wives and children were raped; whose loved ones—and perhaps they themselves—were tortured; who witnessed the shocking brutality of the bombs falling on the cities, of the rockets falling on the houses, and killing children and the elderly, and who, with the shots still ringing in their ears and with the blood still before their eyes, came to power. The natural reaction would be to gun down everyone who lived by the gun. Yet the overwhelming majority of murderous Guardsmen were spared; only an insignificant proportion were shot. We ourselves don't know who was responsible. I'd guess it was as in *Fuenteovejuna*, with everyone in it together.[2]

At the time of the revolutionary triumph, I was given money to begin the work of the ministry of the interior. I started by distributing this money among the police and state security without even asking for receipts. There was no order, no control over anything. We didn't have even the slightest idea what was going on in this country at the time. I don't even know who was in charge of the *La Pólvora* barracks at that moment, and I don't think anyone knows, for people were spending one week in one location and the next in another.

Well, all right, it's possible that if we were to make an investigation we could determine who was responsible at *La Pólvora*. But would we have the moral right to punish those who had fought at the side of the people against the tyranny, who had risked their lives, who had perhaps been wounded, whose parents, siblings, children may have been murdered? By what moral authority are we to ask for sanctions against those people when one considers that there were no control mechanisms—either judicial or military—in effect at the time, that the *compañeros* did not have a clear idea of what they were to do, and may have thought that what they were doing was the policy of the revolution? The communications media upon which we rely to transmit our new way of thinking had not yet been developed.

It would be very difficult for us to determine responsibility for what happened in the first few months after victory—very difficult. We would be demagogues and liars if we were to tell you that we will punish those *compañeros*, if we were to tell you that we will conduct an in-depth investigation to establish who was guilty of the killings that took place in the days immediately following victory.

PUNISHMENT OF ABUSES

On the other hand, we have punished many persons. When we've learned of an infraction, we have penalized those responsible for it, though without publicity, so that I can no longer recall the names of those we've punished. We deported a South American combatant, whose name escapes me, whom we found committing abuses. We promptly expelled him from the country. We likewise jailed the *compañeros* we found committing abuses. I don't know if they have yet been released.

You have no idea what it was like here in the first months of the revolution. There wasn't the least control over anything. When we founded the ministry of the interior we were only six men, and there was not a single policeman, no state security. There were no judges, no tribunals, no supreme court, no anything at all. There were no more than nominations: "you are minister of the interior, you are president of the supreme court of justice." There was no infrastructure. We didn't even have offices. There were no files. There was absolutely nothing.

All we could do at that time was to go from place to place trying to forestall abuses. When they tried to lynch the prisoners who were in the Red Cross building, I personally went over there to talk to the relatives of our martyrs who were seeking revenge. I had to make an extraordinary effort of persuasion. I did not taperecord what I said, but I think it was one of the most eloquent moments of my life, among the few eloquent things I've said in my life. So that I was actually able to persuade them to desist. Ismael Reyes, a member of the Red Cross, was present at the time, for it was he who called me when the crowd began breaking down the doors to get inside and lynch all the murderers within. And we were able to convince them by saying that we could not kill, because we carried out this revolution in order to bring an end to massacres. This was perhaps the most persuasive argument. I asked them, "to what end did we carry out this revolution if we are going to repeat what they did? In that case we would be better off never having undertaken this revolution." We have said the same to the police, to the members of state security, to the *compañeros* of the army: "do not commit abuses, do not be disrespectful of anyone, do not beat prisoners." Because many times they would beat or kill prisoners, and we would say to them: "if you do this, to what end did we carry out the revolution?"

PRISON CONDITIONS

It has been a great struggle, an enormous struggle, for which we have sought the aid of the church, as we have sought the aid of the church in improving prison conditions. A German theologian who expressed admiration for this revolution came to this very office [in the ministry of the interior] and asked me how his church could help. We replied that we'd like them to help us improve conditions for the prisoners. We don't like to say this publicly, although on a few occasions it has slipped out. It is not popular with our people, because if you were Nicaraguan and had been a victim of all that Nicaraguans had suffered, you wouldn't have much sympathy for the idea of improving conditions for the prisoners. When we ask Nicaraguans what they want us to do with the prisoners, they say "shoot them." If we had wanted to please our people, we would have executed them. That is why we asked the theologian and his associates for help in improving conditions for the prisoners. They are going to send us resources. We said to them: "Don't send us resources for our children, who are the ones we love most; send them for the prisoners, for the criminals, for the murderers in the jails."

When Christian businessmen—U.S. millionaires—visited here (among them lunar astronaut Charles Duke) and asked us in what way we would want them to help us, we likewise responded: "Build us the best and most humane prison in Latin America, because we would like to set an example in the treatment of prisoners." They made promises, and we'll see if they keep them. I hope so, because they gave me the impression of being serious and responsible persons. For the time being they have sent us seven thousand bibles, which we have distributed among the prisoners.

Our prisons have serious limitations. There are but a few of them and they are in bad condition, with crowding and food shortages. The guards suffer from these conditions as well. On one occasion I almost started crying, not for the prisoners but for the *compañeros* who were taking care of the prisoners. The *compañeros* looked like the prisoners, and the prisoners looked like those who were taking care of them. The prisoners were better off: our *compañeros* were sleeping on the floor, half-naked, barefoot, dying of hunger. It was a pathetic sight.

This is a country that was left in ruins. The constraints we face are mind-boggling. Even so we are making efforts to improve conditions for the prisoners. It isn't easy, because we have to struggle not only to improve their physical conditions, but also to counter the hatred that is felt for them. We are the ones doing the struggling because we have the moral authority to do so. Had we been National Guardsmen or *somocistas* or indifferent, we would have little moral authority with which to ask the *compañeros* to treat prisoners well. But we were ourselves victims of the National Guard, subjected to torture, to the victimization of our families. That is why we have the authority to tell them to treat the prisoners well, without anyone being able to say we have a personal stake in the matter, because if we were to have any selfish interest, it would be in treating the prisoners poorly.

Certain improvements could be made. We could reduce crowding by building other prisons. With this in mind, we went ahead and built a new prison, spending a million and a half cordobas. But when it was completed we discovered that the engineer who planned the construction—an incompetent for sure—had forgotten to make provision for sewers, and other experts then determined that because of ground conditions it would be impossible to install sewers on that site. All our efforts of several months, motivated by the great hope of being able to transfer those prisoners so they could live in better conditions (we had already planned conjugal visits and other elemental things we intended to introduce in the new penitentiary system), were laid low.

Now we need to begin searching for other sites to build a prison, which will take several more months. The inspector has said we cannot transfer anyone else to Granada. In the meantime we have given instructions to permit more frequent visitations.

Yesterday I was in the Jinotepe jail and found we are in need of better communication. We still haven't perfected our channels of communication. The order to permit more frequent visitations had not arrived; nor had the order to allow the prisoners books, periodicals, and so forth. We even had to release some prisoners held unjustly.

We are fully disposed to increasing the number of visits allowed prisoners. Keep in mind that there are administrative problems involved here. The Tipitapa jail, for example, was designed for seven hundred prisoners but holds over two thousand. That makes it more difficult for the *compañeros* to regulate the visits, which means we have to augment personnel, which is costly. But we have authorized more frequent visitations, just as we have authorized prisoners to walk freely about the halls, to receive books, newspapers, magazines, cigarettes, radio, television, and other things that had been denied them, like lemons, oranges, and other kinds of fruit. All this has now been put into effect.

On a visit to the Granada prison, I discovered that the *compañeros* of the penitentiary system had put into effect a rather mechanical and even childish regulation, stipulating that every time an official went by, the prisoners had to rise to attention. One of the staff members, Leana, passed back and forth three hundred times a day, and every time she went by, all the women had to stand at attention. It was ridiculous. We still haven't straightened out all such problems, much less perfected our administrative mechanisms, though we've made progress.

We're going to release more prisoners. Many have already been released. Unfortunately we have made the mistake of not publicizing the penalties we have applied against many *compañeros* for maltreatment of prisoners, just as we have failed to adequately publicize the number of prisoners we have freed, which runs into the thousands. The only publicity was in the first days after the triumph, when I released over a hundred prisoners in Jinotega. These were ex-Guardsmen who—by the way—are now among the "disappeared," having taken off for Honduras.

We're going to release all those whose physical condition precludes their being dangerous, unless the charges against them are particularly serious. And we're going to send lawyers to the jails to investigate the possibilities of freeing more prisoners. In December we will issue pardons. We will review the case of each prisoner. We will release all who are physically disabled, as well as those who are clearly not guilty. We will also review sentences handed out in the first few months, many of which may have been excessive, in which case they will have to be reduced.[3]

It isn't easy to figure out who's telling the truth and who isn't. Many of the prisoners have gone so far as to adopt pseudonyms. When their families come looking for them, they "cannot be found." They are very fearful of the revolution, fearful of their own crimes. They have guilt complexes, which is why they won't give us their true names. What's more, if you take a look at the answers they give in the special tribunals, you'll see that they were all cooks, typists, street sweepers, barbers, mechanics. Not one of them fired a shot. It would appear that we shot ourselves. Some say: "I was recruited only three days before my capture." Others say they had been in the army only one month, or had deserted, or that they were with the *Frente Sandinista*. Uncovering the truth in all these cases is very difficult.

We are, however, preparing groups of *compañeros*, whom we've been instructing in legal principles, in respect for human rights, in courtroom technique, to speed up the trials. This was a big problem at first, but we are becoming more experienced in these procedures with each passing day, and another thirty-five *compañeros* are being trained.

As I was saying, it's a difficult process. We had no experience in these matters. Who had been the judges in this country? Who had acquired judicial experience? The *somocistas*, and within a framework of corruption. We on the other hand learned how to fight; we are still halfway guerrilla fighters. We had no legal experience. None of us were judges, prosecutors, police, or anything of the sort. We have had to learn on the job.

It has been barely over a year since the triumph, which in historical perspective is a mere instant. In fact, we've barely begun to put together a government. Though we would like to develop our party, the *Frente Sandinista*, it has had to wait as we address the primary task of organizing a government. The 19th of July [anniversary of the revolutionary triumph] came along this year and we still hadn't begun to concern ourselves with the *Frente Sandinista* as a political organization. Why? Because our priorities were with health, the literacy campaign, and defense of the revolution, and now that these are in place we've had to proceed to give the judicial system the attention it deserves. Until recently they didn't even have a building or a vehicle; now they've been given a building and vehicles, they've been given a boost, and we meet with them frequently. We didn't get around to it sooner because we had more pressing matters to attend to.

PLURALISM AND A MIXED ECONOMY

The removal of Somoza's tyrannical regime likewise entailed the removal of the legal and coercive instruments of *somocismo* that sustained it. It was not only a matter of reconstructing buildings destroyed by the war, but of reconstructing the state apparatus, at least as difficult a task.

Some Nicaraguans are nervous about what is happening, but it must be emphasized that there has been a revolution here. And a revolution makes some very happy and others unhappy; some feel secure and others insecure. The overwhelming majority of Nicaraguans, formerly threatened, have now regained a sense of security. They were living in extreme insecurity, because they were among the ones being killed, imprisoned, tortured, dispossessed, and because they didn't have access to work, to education, to anything. But who was responsible for this insecurity? The social classes that dominated this country. Now those who formerly lived in fear feel secure for the first time; but those who formerly were responsible for the insecurity of the immense majority now feel insecure, in spite of the fact that this revolution has been flexible enough to provide opportunity for all, and even though we have seriously proposed—not just tactically or for a short time—a mixed economy and political pluralism.

We are serious when we speak of political pluralism and a mixed economy. But what is happening is that thieves think everyone shares their outlook on life. So they think we are deceiving them, when much of our effort has gone into trying to persuade them that we are not liars, and that historically speaking it is they who have been the liars. They cannot conceive of the possibility that there might be others who are not liars, and they feel insecure. Obviously, it's a vicious circle, because the very insecurity they have fallen into leads them to decapitalize their businesses, weakening their sector of the economy.

And when they begin to decapitalize, the workers become aware of what they are doing, and then the revolution becomes concerned in the matter. We are not prepared to let them decapitalize their enterprises; this country cannot afford their lack of confidence. The simplest proof [of their decapitalization] is that they are all in debt to our financial system [having transferred dollars borrowed on credit for the purpose of developing their businesses to bank accounts in Miami and Switzerland]. And the revolution could say to them—not even as a radical measure, but as a matter of standard business practice—"either pay up on your debts or we take over the businesses as collateral." And what has the revolution done? Has it taken over these businesses? No. On the contrary it has extended them more loans for development.

PRIVATE PROPERTY

Unfortunately, we have a backward bourgeoisie. I think in the long run a sector of the so-called private enterprise in our country will become stablilized, a sector that will acquire a measure of common sense. There are even some foolish ones who may yet acquire that common sense. Note that we could have simply seized their holdings; we have the power to do so. Yet had we done so, we would have shown as little sense as they do. But we have learned something from history. We have realized that to be revolutionaries, to carry forth a revolution, we have to keep our feet on the ground. I am certain we could expropriate the large landholders and businessmen without being overthrown. But what is proper for the economic development of this country is determined by what is best for the common good of Nicaraguans. We are serious when we speak of a mixed economy, just as when we speak of political pluralism. The maintenance of a mixed economy and political pluralism conforms with the political agenda of the *Frente Sandinista*. We are not going to violate our principles. But we cannot allow businesses to be decapitalized, because to decapitalize them means to destroy them and transfer resources outside the country.

We intend to develop private industry, private commerce, and private cultivation of the land. What's more, we are not interested in nationalizing the land. On the contrary, we are interested in expanding private ownership of land. We'd like this to be primarily in the form of cooperatives, but we are also interested in developing some of the existing agricultural enterprises. We will give them all the assistance necessary, as we have done with the San Antonio sugar mill, for example, which is a multimillion-dollar business in private hands.

We will multiply the number of cooperatives, which are an entirely voluntary form of private landownership. There is nothing strange or collectivist about cooperatives, as some backward elements here think, who haven't the slightest idea what a cooperative is. One need only read half a page from a book on the subject to realize that a cooperative involves private ownership.

POLITICAL PARTIES AND ELECTIONS

There is political uncertainty in some sectors, which stands to reason when you consider that the traditional parties of this country have ruled Nicaragua for over a hundred years without resolving its problems. Yet these parties want to keep on living, and stubbornly refuse to consign themselves to the museum. We will not interfere with their continued existence; they will die a natural death to make way for the emergence of new, modern, different political parties. . . .

On a particular occasion when they demanded immediate elections, we said no because, among other things, we are advocates of political pluralism. If we had held elections six months after the victory—or at this very moment—they wouldn't be representative; political pluralism would disappear. If the legislature had one hundred representatives, it would be a legislature of one hundred Sandinistas. And because we believe in pluralism, we're going to wait for them to gain some political space, to organize through some party, so they may meaningfully present themselves as a choice.

Besides, we cannot afford to waste time in an electoral process at this moment. It would be a waste of effort, energy, and resources at a time when the priority is to reactivate our economy. But elections will be held within a fixed length of time—we've already indicated a date.[4] That will be the appropriate time for an electoral contest, but not for debating whether or not there is a revolution in Nicaragua.

A COMMITMENT TO TRUTH

We have publicly criticized persons in the business sector, but they have criticized us as well. They demand the right to attack us, but do not accept our right to attack them. If they can attack us, why can't we do the same in reverse? If they call us communists, why can't we call them reactionaries? If they say we've been bought by the gold of Moscow, why can't we say they've prostituted themselves to imperialism? If they have the same right to free speech as we do, and they attack us in *La Prensa* and on *Radio Corporación* and other radio stations, then we can attack them in our own communications media. . . .

It is true that some means of communication, like *Radio Sandino*, belong to the *Frente Sandinista*, just as *Radio Corporación* belongs to the reactionaries. Some other mass communications media, like the television system, are in the hands of the government. I would like you to ask the French why they hold major communications media in the hands of the state. Television, for example, is government-run in France, just as it is in Spain and Nicaragua. The way this came about in Nicaragua was that Somoza owned the television system, and all that had been Somoza's passed into the hands of the new power in this country. If there had been a private television channel, it would have continued in private hands.

We do not now favor authorizing a new private television channel, because we are making efforts to transform our television. Traditionally, television has been alienating—because it has promoted pornographic films that exalt crime and other deformities. We are trying to transform television into something educational, because television is a very effective medium of communication.

We could, however, consider providing access to television for other components of society—the church, for example. We are not averse to the idea that the church have access to television. The Human Rights Commission headed by Dr. Leonte Herdocia has made such a request.

We have found it is much better to tell the truth, because it entails fewer problems than telling lies. In fact there is an advantage in *always* telling the truth. The natural tendency, however, is to try to conceal mistakes, and to exaggerate. Once when we were prisoners, the Red Cross arrived to speak with the *compañeros.* Despite our usual straightforwardness—for such has been the Sandinista tradition—*compañeros* exaggerated, some of them making up stories.

I will tell you something that will show you to what point our sense of honesty leads us. We have admitted that the prisoners in the Tipitapa jail are subject to worse conditions than the ones we experienced. Our conditions were better. How's that? Because in Tipitapa we were allowed visits once a week, and at times there were odd occurrences. One day they wouldn't let me have a book on mental energy, thinking it could help me escape; another day they allowed me to receive [Karl Marx's] *El Capital*, saying, "this can be allowed in, because it's on capitalism." (We have permitted entry of any reading materials with the exception of comics and pornography.) But we experienced better conditions. Not I perhaps, because I was placed in an isolation cell, but the great majority of the *compañeros* were better off. This is in large measure attributable to the number of prisoners. There were far fewer then, and obviously it is easier to care for a small number than for a large number.[5]

When we were imprisoned at the site you visited, over in El Chipote, we were kept with hoods over our heads, handcuffed, and were beaten every day. We hoped to be transferred to Tipitapa, because to us Tipitapa was almost like being freed. There was such a violent contrast that going to Tipitapa was like being let out on the street. Now the opposite is true. Those who are in El Chipote do not want to go to Tipitapa, and those who are at Tipitapa would like to go back to El Chipote. They'd rather be in the state security detention facility because with fewer prisoners it's less uncomfortable than Tipitapa, and they can prepare their own meals, eat what they want to. Not so in Tipitapa, where conditions are much harsher. . . .

It was very difficult to take action against all who committed abuses in the period right after the triumph. We had enough prisoners as it was without adding in our own people. If we'd imprisoned all those who committed abuses, I think we'd have half a million Nicaraguans in jail. Because cars were being stolen, houses were being sacked—all those that were unoccupied. There wasn't a single house spared. Who was looting them? The people, our *compañeros*, members of our army. Incredible things happened in our country.

It seemed only natural to them to remove everything they could get their hands on, as though it were collective property. They did us great economic harm by sacking and damaging houses. In this very building they took away all but the roof; air conditioners, toilets were ripped out. The Montealegre house on the Southern Highway was taken apart. We wanted the house maintained intact; it contained a fortune in chinaware alone. It had belonged to a millionaire who spent three million cordobas on his daughter's wedding. It was a beauty. Such houses should be preserved, for they belong to the people. So we assigned some *compañeros* to watch over it. I arrived a month later to see how things were going, and there was nothing left. They said to me: "Someone came from the Ministry of Culture saying you gave him permission to remove the contents." I doubt he was from the Ministry of Culture. It was considered the most normal thing in the world to walk off with things. This is called pillaging, it is called robbing, and is forbidden by law all around the world. I chanced upon a broken painting, dragged across the ground: it was a Picasso. I was able to confirm that it was authentic, but the pillager had no interest in Picasso. So I doubt he was from the Ministry of Culture; and if he was, he was ignorant.

INCREDIBLE ABUSES

This is what happened; there was no control over anything. In the early days following the triumph our people would seize a car, use it until it ran out of gasoline, then abandon it and seize another.

In this manner a great number of luxury cars, Mercedes-Benzes, were destroyed in accidents. They'd get out of the wrecked car, stop an oncoming driver, make him get out, and off they'd go with his car. If they came upon a parked car, they'd seize it. And they'd race about at incredible speeds, causing more accidents and deaths.

We understood the psychological meaning of all this. For the first time our people felt in control of their own country, a country that had been alien, that had not been ours; it had been a foreign country. We had been strangers in our own country, discriminated against by its masters who weren't any of us. Now for the first time our people felt in charge of their own country, and of the streets and highways, and began killing each other by speeding around like lunatics. And they began to take for themselves all that had always been denied them. Persons who had never had anything all of a sudden felt they owned everything. They did great damage to the economy of the country, but there was no way to prevent it.

We were successful only in keeping them from killing the ex-Guardsmen. They killed some, but nothing like the numbers they could have. Had we given the slightest sign of approval, not a single ex-Guardsman would have been left alive in this country; had we yielded just a little, they would have all been dead. But we were stern and unbending so as not only to prevent our people from killing, but also from maltreating, the prisoners—which we were able to achieve insofar as possible. It was a major historical achievement, because we prepared ourselves for it under Carlos Fonseca's guidance, because this revolution taught itself to respect others. And we also did it in the awareness that if we carried out a bloody revolution here, with firing squads and physical maltreatment, we would make things more difficult for revolutionaries in other countries, damaging their possibilities of forming alliances, and frightening people all over. . . .

Just as we couldn't prevent the looting or send those responsible for it to jail, neither could we prevent the killing of a number of prisoners or the maltreatment of some others; we couldn't prevent it. Who did it? It isn't known; it was "the people," the same people who sacked the country. This same people did the killings—a people who had for so long lived in disgraceful conditions. There was an explosion here, which was kept from being much larger thanks to the good sense, maturity, and respect for human dignity imparted by the leaders of this revolution.

Just as we made the decision to respect human rights, we made the decision to invite you here and grant you full freedom of movement, despite some reservations, because we weren't sure the commission would act with the necessary objectivity and understanding. You probably also had some prejudices about us. But we see that you have a positive attitude and that you don't intend to place us in the dock of the accused, but rather intend to stimulate us in our decision to respect human rights.

But we would like to go a step beyond that, to become a shining example of respect for human rights on this continent, and we will achieve this aim. So that when the words "human rights" are uttered, when human rights are spoken of, it will be said, "as in Nicaragua." You can help us in this.

NOTES

1. For independent documentation of Borge's charges against the *contras*, see Reed Brody, *Contra Terror in Nicaragua* (Boston: South End Press, 1985).

2. *Fuenteovejuna* is the name of a village in a play by Spanish poet and dramatist Lope Félix de Vega Carpio. In the play all the residents take responsibility for murdering the king's oppressive tax collector.

3. The last four sentences of this paragraph have been relocated from elsewhere in the original in order to improve organization and readability.

4. Elections were promised for 1985, and were in fact held on November 4, 1984. Contrary to predictions of a Soviet-style plebiscitary sham, opposition parties ranging from communist to conservative garnered one-third of the vote and 35 of 96 seats in the National Assembly. They later obtained 10 of 22 seats on the Constitutional Commission appointed to draft a new constitution. Even this understates the degree of pluralism; the FSLN chose many nonparty members to represent it in the National Assembly, and no fewer than four of the twelve FSLN delegates on the Constitutional Commission are explictly Christian revolutionaries.

5. It was not standard practice for Somoza's National Guard to take prisoners, except among the upper classes. As in Guatemala and El Salvador today, extra-judicial murders and "disappearances" predominated.

4

The Revolutionary Aim:
To Eliminate Sin, Not Sinners
(1981)

What follows is the text of Borge's March 5, 1981 address to a conference on the ministry in Latin America organized by the Evangelical churches in Nicaragua and held at the Polytechnic University, Managua.

After sketching the history of the prophetic church in Nicaragua and addressing the issue of religious freedom, Borge develops one of his principal religious themes: that of pardoning one's enemies in order to eradicate sin, not sinners. In the process, he relates the story of his encounter with his wife's murderer.

The theme of mercy is then grounded in a comprehensive view of human rights, most particularly in a right to life that rules out torture and capital punishment, and encompasses rights to the necessities of life, including food, education, and love.

Borge was preceded at the podium by Rev. José María Ruiz, an octagenarian Baptist minister in Managua, who was later elected to the National Assembly (the Nicaraguan legislature) on the FSLN ticket in November 1984.

I am deeply moved by Reverend Ruiz's presentation. Much of what I've been intending to say has already been said by this at once venerable elder and extraordinary youth.

DOING AWAY WITH SELFISHNESS

What is the fundamental objective of the revolution? It is, as the Reverend Ruiz indicated, to achieve human liberation. And achieving human liberation encompasses more than the attainment of social justice, more than eradicating illiteracy and ignorance. We cannot limit ourselves to building highways. For though someday we will fulfill our old dream of erecting dwellings for everyone, and sometime—perhaps very soon—we will wipe out unemployment, all this is no more than one aspect of human liberation.

The key to human liberation is in the words we've just heard. So long as we don't set selfishness aside, we will not have achieved human liberation, and will not have fulfilled our revolutionary dreams. Only when human beings live for each other and not for themselves alone—when they are able to open the floodgates of their hearts and give fully of themselves to others—only on that day will we have completed the revolution.

We have already taken an important step in that direction, by overthrowing the Herods, the Caligulas. We have dismantled that anachronistic, aberrant, and unjust system, and we are seeking to create a new society, a society whose essence consists of faith in the future and in love. This is the society we intend to construct, and when we say its essence is love, we mean generosity, the capacity to give fully of oneself and to eradicate selfishness. So our present struggle, building on the struggle against the past, against *somocismo*, is the struggle against selfishness. And if yesterday we overthrew Somoza, tomorrow—sometime—we will overthrow selfishness.

We have sought to educate our *militantes* in this spirit, emphasizing that every Sandinista should be an example in everyday life. We have conceived of the organization [the FSLN] as a vanguard, so as to place the best sons and daughters of our country at the front of—though not on top of—the people. Immersed among the people, integrated with the people, but at the head of the people in their spirit of sacrifice, in self-denial, in revolutionary modesty, in unaffectedness, and—if necessary—in readiness to die on behalf of this people and its revolution.

On occasion it has been said that our revolution restores humanity to human beings. For human beings have been dehumanized, converted into instruments of consumption, subjected to propaganda, and made instruments of powerful interests that are enemies of humaneness. The revolution is precisely a response to the alienation to which human beings have been subjected, but at the same time it gives rise to its opposite, the counterrevolution. In all of history there has never been a single case of a revolution without a simultaneous counterrevolution, and no sector of society is spared from this historical law.

In the Christian churches that form one segment of society, there are a great many revolutionaries, and among them church leaders, who fully identify with the interests of the people. But there are others who prefer to long for the past than face the future. Some hold to—in their words—the "American way of life" as their model of society. They're the ones who worship the golden calf, the very ones Christ once drove out of the temple with a whip. They're the ones who denounce the literacy crusade, the voluntary work of the people, the reconstruction of the country in its various aspects, as totalitarian measures.

But there is a new church that is identified with the people. In the case of Protestants, this commitment to place themselves on the side of the people is grounded in biblical study of the prophets of social justice, like Amos, and in the example of the German theologian Dietrich Bonhoeffer, who was—as you surely know—a great battler against fascism, against German Nazism. In Nicaragua it can be said that the committed sectors of the church, among them Protestants, were influenced and stimulated by this theologian and his militancy in the resistance against Nazism.

A CENTER OF CONSPIRACY AGAINST EVIL

What is the church if not the community of the faithful? The church is not a building; it's not a cathedral that can be easily destroyed, as was the cathedral of Managua (along with other church buildings) by the [1972] earthquake. The church consists of human beings who hold a particular conception of the world, a particular belief, a faith. This is the church that fought against the Somoza dictatorship.

I understand there are fourteen Latin American countries represented here: Colombia, Venezuela, Mexico, Ecuador, Peru, Argentina, Chile, Uruguay, Paraguay, and others. It is well that Latin American Christians should know that Nicaraguan Christians— that is to say, the church—fought against Somoza's tyranny. It is well that you should know—surely you have already heard it—that thousands upon thousands of Catholic, Protestant, and other Christians fought in all aspects of the struggle. And that they did not fight only with prayer, or by invoking Christ's name, for they also fought in the trenches and behind the barricades.

The people, this rebellious and combative people, congregated in the churches. The churches became a center of conspiracy against evil—a center of respect for righteousness—because when one conspires against evil, one renders homage to righteousness. It was in this way that Christians in Nicaragua worshiped the man who was crucified two thousand years ago.

"CHRISTIANS" WHO NEVER WERE CHRISTIANS

Other "Christians," with their musty souls, like to fondle Christ for their personal interests and privileges. And with more than just words, for when words are divorced from actions they lack meaning. Today, in this new stage of the revolution, we see how the pharisees, the profaners of the temple, are beating their chests and have all of a sudden become fervent devotees of Christ the King.

They have never been Christians. Never! Regardless of the fact that from a formal standpoint they identified themselves as Catholics on their passports or other public documents where they were to designate their religion; and regardless of their coming very well dressed and perfumed to Mass on Sundays, to deposit their miserable alms and show off the latest fashions. Regardless of all this, they were never Christians! And today it turns out that a large number of new Christians have appeared on the scene, who are Christians of the old stamp—meaning, Christians who are new from the standpoint of time but not from the standpoint of their Christian character. . . .

FROM VALDIVIESO TO GASPAR GARCÍA LAVIANA

We will not forget the example set by young Christians during the struggle against Somoza, not only in the eastern barrios [of Managua], but in the whole country; though especially in the eastern barrios. Do you remember when they took over the University of Central America to obtain the release of prisoners? And the sit-ins organized in churches throughout Nicaragua; the participation of Catholics and Protestants in the experience of Solentiname [Father Ernesto Cardenal's contemplative community of fisherfolk and farmers on islands in Lake Cocibolca] and—with the Maryknoll Sisters—in Estelí and in Barrio Sandino, where one of the martyrs in El Salvador [Maura Clarke, one of four U.S. churchwomen raped and murdered by the Salvadoran military on Dec. 2, 1980] had been. I believe Camilo Torres, a Colombian priest, inspired these Christians.[1]

Pastoral workers have begun to restore the spirit of the church by rededicating it to serve the humble and exploited, a tradition bequeathed us in Nicaragua by Fray Antonio de Valdivieso and by Simón Pereira Castellón, bishop of León. The former was murdered for his love of the Amerindians, because he had dedicated himself to the cause of the Amerindians enslaved and tortured by the Spanish colonialists; the latter denounced U.S. intervention in Nicaragua [against Sandino between 1927 and 1933] in his sermons.

Perhaps the greatest practical expression of Christian belief in Nicaragua is in the immortal example of the priest Gaspar García Laviana [who gave his life to the revolution as a Sandinista *comandante*]. And among Protestants, the Salvadoran Reverend Augusto Cotto, a Baptist pastor whose commitment to the Latin American struggle was enormous.[2] In El Salvador there's the great priest, patriot, crusader, and martyr, Bishop Oscar Romero.

Today, following the triumph of the revolution, the Christian people of Nicaragua continue to be immersed in the struggle for tomorrow, laboring to create a new society; not just physically, not just to raise buildings—which is important—but also to reconstruct the moral fiber of human life, which is in my judgment the most important aspect of national reconstruction.

I should like to acknowledge and highlight the participation and effort of certain Protestant organizations, among them FUMEC, the Ecumenical Axis of Nicaragua, CELADEC, the World Council of Churches, the National Council of Churches of the United States, the Protestant churches of Germany, Sweden, and the socialist countries, and the Christian Conference for Peace.[3] All of these labor in an extraordinarily valuable terrain for the reconstruction of our country.

RELIGIOUS FREEDOM

There are many pastors here. Has anyone—for I am not aware of any such instance—ever interfered with your religious observances in Nicaragua? Have there been hindrances to the exercise of your religious beliefs? Tell me candidly. Because if there has been some restraint, some obstacle, we are prepared to defend your right to render homage to Christ. I see that no one is saying there have been interferences, so I must suppose there haven't been any.

All the same, there are some who say there is no religious freedom in Nicaragua. What's more, others say we are trying to instrumentalize religion. We know that a traditional Nicaraguan Catholic procession normally held in early January was canceled to prevent us from taking part in it, because we had participated in the activities of the feast of St. Dominic [patron saint of Managua], and other religious festivities. Regardless of our religious beliefs, let us suppose all Sandinistas were atheists. I want to emphasize we are *not* all atheists, because many Sandinistas are Christians. But let's suppose we were philosophically atheist and that in spite of that fact we were to join in a religious celebration. Who can deprive us of the right to be present with the people? Don't we have the right to participate in these traditional festivities?

I understand many of you, by reason of your religious beliefs, do not agree with the veneration of saints. But all right, here in Nicaragua we have a religious celebration known as *La Purísima*. It may be that from a philosophical point of view we would see this celebration in a particular light, or that from a biblical point of view we would see it in another light, but doesn't it happen to be a beautiful celebration that brings joy to the hearts of Nicaraguans? Why should we deny ourselves the right to participate in the joys of our people?

Neither do we deny the right of anyone to participate in the revolutionary joy of our people. Whom have we denied the right to come to the Plaza de la Revolución or the Plaza 19 de Julio, when the people celebrate revolutionary holidays? Haven't we invited even the top hierarchs of the Catholic Church? I think from now on we should invite not only the Catholics but also the Protestants, who have every right to participate as religious representatives in the patriotic and revolutionary celebrations in our country. It seems to me they have that right, and moreover they are earning it.

All the same, it is said there is no religious freedom in Nicaragua. Although all here have the right to exercise their religious beliefs, many citizens of the U.S.A. return to their country to parrot the slogans preached by the enemies of the revolution, the acolytes of imperialism, and the *vendepatria* bourgeoisie [the bourgeoisie that would gladly "sell" its own "homeland"]. They try to convert the church into a carrier pigeon flying into the past, even though carrier pigeons fly only toward the future. Surely some of them long for the time when our people suffered so. Nicaraguans should recount to the *compañeros* from other countries—surely they've done so—what we suffered here: the tortures, the murders, the aerial bombings. There isn't a family—and I say this above all for the *compañeros* of other nations—that hasn't been a victim of *somocista* crime.

There are those who make the rounds of other countries saying we are burning churches. Such is their propaganda: that we would be church-burners. The truth is that this people that suffered so much is fully respected by the revolution, as are its religious sentiments. What's more, many of the virtues we consider vital to a revolutionary coincide fully with Christian virtues.

THE BIBLE IN THE JAILS

When seven thousand bibles arrived from some Christians in the United States, I said: "Give them to the prisoners." Because common sense and the logic of history inform us that Christian principles assist in elevating moral character. You, for example, as I understand it, are austere in your personal lives, which is good. And surely the Bible will help these criminals, torturers, murderers.

It is good that pastors visit the prisons, because, if I am not mistaken, Christ did not come for the righteous but for the sinners. And the greatest sinners this country has had are in jail for the sin of having fought against the people, which is the worst of sins, because, I believe, to sin against the people and its interests is to sin against the Holy Spirit.

SERVING TWO MASTERS?

We know—I said I would speak frankly—of some Protestant pastors who slander the revolution abroad. And—what a coincidence!—some of them are the very same persons who are blessing [Paraguayan dictator Alfredo] Stroessner and blessing the genocide against the Salvadoran people. Some are perhaps even among those who designated [Anastasio] Somoza [García] "prince of the church." They are brought together by the same common denominator. And we ask ourselves, to which church do they answer? To the church of the scepters adorned with diamonds, of the thrones inlaid with gold, to which Reverend Ruiz referred, the church of the rich (because today all the rich in this country have become great churchgoers)? Or the church of the poor? To which church?

One cannot serve two masters, as Reverend Ruiz reminded us. One cannot love in general, but only in particular. One cannot love the oppressed without confronting oppressors. I'm not saying you shouldn't love oppressors, but to love oppressors one must sometimes strike them. Sometimes even revolutionary repression is a form of love from a Christian point of view. Yes, it's true someone has said that you cannot love the exploited without hating the exploiters, but all right, we can take hold of this phrase and say that this "hate" expressed in practical terms is no more than a higher form of love. Because when exploiters destroy, torture, or murder, and we revolutionaries confront them and remove them from circulation, in one way or another we are doing good to those guilty of doing evil, we are purifying them, trying to convert them into something different from what they are.

OUR REVENGE: TO PARDON OUR ENEMIES

What are we doing in the prisons? I once said: "We are not interested in destroying sinners, but in eliminating sin." And what are we doing with these murderers? We are trying to convert them into what they have never been: true human beings. That's what we're attempting to do, and I believe it is our moral obligation to raise them from their condition as beasts to the condition of human beings.

That is the philosophy of our revolution. And clearly, they don't understand. When I was a prisoner I would speak with them of these things, and would tell them that someday we would help them, and yet they wouldn't believe it, and they still doubt it. I remember it had been a few days since they'd captured my wife's murderer. When that man saw me (they had savagely tortured her, had raped her, had ripped out her fingernails), he thought—who knows what?—that he was going to be killed, or that he was going to be beaten at the least. He was absolutely astonished when I arrived before him and treated him like a human being. He couldn't understand it, nor can he understand it even now, and perhaps he will never understand it. As we've said from time to time: "our revenge toward our enemies will be to pardon them; it's the best of revenges."

HUMAN RIGHTS: DEFENDING LIFE

Some have attacked us on the question of human rights. They say there are eighty-five hundred political prisoners here. They say we engage in torture. I think you have the wisdom and common sense to understand that these assertions aren't just simple slanders but part of a plan to provoke distrust in the revolutionary process.

We have said we intend to convert Nicaragua into a showcase, an example of human rights, and we will achieve this aim. To be sure, when we speak of human rights, we don't mean only treatment of prisoners, because there are some who think that human rights encompass no more than not mistreating a prisoner, not killing someone. That is far too simplistic.

We believe that the defense of human rights is the defense of the rights of the people, of the right to life. The capacity to give love without expecting anything in return—*that* is generosity, and the day when we have a society in which all live for others—where all radiate love of others through word and deed—on that day we will have achieved the society toward which we aspire; the completion, the archetype, of a society characterized by respect for human rights, because a society of generous persons cannot disrespect the dignity of a human being.

Conversely, there can hardly be respect for human rights in a country where children suffer from hunger. There can hardly be respect for human rights in any country where children don't go to school. There can hardly be respect for human rights in any part of the world where children don't receive love, and love in practical terms is also bread and education.

Mural of Luis Alfonso Velásquez in the church of San Francisco de los Angeles, Barrio Riguero, Managua. Though only a child, Luis organized Christian resistance to the Somoza regime in Barrio Riguero, explaining that the passivity of the older generation required action by youth. The National Guard shot him in the head, then ran him over, killing him at the age of nine.

I'm not going to say there is no torture here. Why shall I say that if we are unyielding in confronting those who in any way abuse their authority? With the military person who exercises authority to maltreat another human being, what happens? When we find out what's going on, we are implacable with such persons.

There is not one human being on earth who isn't worthy of

respect, not even those who, like the ones who are in jail, were the murderers of our loved ones. In all the world there isn't a human being who isn't worthy of respect. That includes the great enemies of our peoples, who are objects of our attack, of our struggle, but, as isolated individuals, if they should fall into our hands, if the detested son of Somoza, *el Chigüin*, should fall into our hands, we would be obligated to respect him as a person.[4] Even with such persons so abhorred by the people, we would have the moral and revolutionary obligation of respecting them in their physical integrity, though they would fall under the weight of the law.

TO LIE: TO OFFEND AGAINST HUMAN RIGHTS

It is said there is no freedom of expression in Nicaragua. Yet there is not only freedom of expression but freedom to lie. And to lie is to offend against human rights. Here falsehood has become institutionalized in certain mass media, and perhaps in this sense we are exceedingly tolerant. Is not the struggle of peoples and of human beings for justice likewise a struggle for truth? When falsehood is expressed one must fight it, and there are times when to be tolerant of lies is to be complicit with them.

I think that to this end we need to strengthen the cooperative relationship between the church and the revolution, and that we can take some practical steps: first of all, disseminating the truth. We don't ask anyone to praise the revolution, only to disseminate the truth.

JOINING HANDS WITH THE POOR

I believe it is an obligation of religious congregations, of religious institutions, to participate in the tasks of production. That is to say, to express their commitment to the future, to tomorrow, and to the people in practical terms: in voluntary work, through austerity, by conserving water and electricity, which is so expensive to Nicaragua; in community development through the mass organizations or through Christian institutions; in the literacy campaign and its continuation; in popular culture, sports, and all activities that contribute to the development of our people.

All Nicaraguans, regardless of religious belief, should step forward together, with our hands interlinked as brothers and sisters on the road of the revolution. It matters not that some should be Protestants and others Episcopalians or Catholics: what is important is that all are human beings, and I believe if Christ were to be born and crucified all over again, he would again die for all humankind. On behalf of the poor given priority by Christ, we are ready to commit our life and our blood.

The revolution is on behalf of all human beings, but—as with Christ—above all for the poor. Our revolution was not made to maintain the exploitation of humans by humans, to maintain the privileges of millionaires, but to restore the rights of the humble and the poor. It was no coincidence that Christ chose his apostles from among the poor. There isn't the slightest doubt that Christ died on the cross for the poor. They are the very ones this revolution struggles for, and for whom we are ready to commit our lives and our blood.

NOTES

1. Frustrated in his efforts to effect peaceful reform, Colombian priest and sociologist Camilo Torres joined a revolutionary guerrilla force and was killed in combat in February 1966.

2. Baptist minister Augusto Cotto was killed in a plane crash after having been entrusted with foreign relations for El Salvador's FMLN-FDR opposition government. It is believed a bomb was planted on his plane by agents of the Salvadoran government.

3. FUMEC stands for *Federación Universal de Movimientos Estudiantiles Cristianos,* World Federation of Christian Student Movements. Borge's 1985 address to a FUMEC conference is included in this volume. CELADEC stands for *Comisión Evangélica Latinoamericana de Educación Cristiana,* Latin American Evangelical Commission for Christian Education, based in Lima, Peru.

4. "El Chigüin," Anastasio Somoza Portocarrero, is the eldest son of ex-dictator Anastasio Somoza Debayle. He succeeded his father (and grandfather, Anastasio Somoza García) as commander of the National Guard, and became notorious for his brutality against Nicaragua's civilian population in the last two years of his father's rule. He now lives in Miami.

5

What It Means to Be a Sandinista (1981)

This speech was addressed to Sandinistas gathered in Niquino-homo, the village of Augusto Sandino's birth, for the installation of party militantes. *The ceremony took place on February 21, 1981, to mark the 47th anniversary of the assassination of Sandino by Anastasio Somoza García, founder of the Somoza dynasty.*

The position of militante *in the Sandinista party is in many ways equivalent to the priesthood in the Catholic Church. It involves far more than what is ordinarily meant by membership, because of the depth of personal commitment signified by acceptance of the position. Like priests,* militantes *are expected to place the interests of society ahead of personal interests (though they may marry). Societal interests are in turn closely associated with the welfare of the organization, which has dedicated itself to those purposes. That means that just as priests are expected to obey their bishops,* militantes *are expected to obey their* comandantes. *And like elevations within the Catholic Church, Sandinista promotions are determined from the top down.*

There are some important differences, though. For one thing, there is no Sandinista pope. The Sandinistas have avoided concentrating charisma in one central figure, as happened in Castro's Cuba, in favor of a nine-person National Directorate. Their leadership is conciliar, with ample internal debate aimed at achieving consensus on major policy decisions.

There are also differences between what is expected of priests and militantes, *although such differences have narrowed for much of the Latin American church as it has committed itself to the "preferential option for the poor." Interestingly, the convergence has not been one-sided. Elsewhere in these selections, we hear Borge telling gatherings of Christians that the moral principles of Sandinism coincide in large measure with those of Christianity. Here, in his "ordination speech" for the first* militantes, *is evidence aplenty.*

"On the fiftieth anniversary of Sandino's assassination,
Sandino lives!" On side of house, Villa Libertad, Managua

Earlier it was announced that this would be the first promotion of cadres in the *Frente Sandinista de Liberación Nacional,* FSLN. Yesterday our National Directorate came to the conclusion that it would be the second promotion. We also decided that this ceremony, in which the first membership cards will be handed out in commemoration of the death of the father of the Popular Anti-Imperialist Revolution, should be carried out in front of the people and with the people, inasmuch as Sandinista *militantes* should be the men and women whom the people places at the vanguard of its historic challenge.

Why isn't this the first promotion? It *is* the first within the new party structures to the FSLN, but is not the first from the point of view of our history. I think Sandinistas of today are sufficiently humble to acknowledge that the first promotion to the status of *militantes* fully belongs to those who earned the seal of revolutionary participation in the middle of the night, in the catacombs, at the edge of fatigue and danger; those who never heard any more than the song of the bird on the mountain, the silence of the underground, and who at last left, bloodied and still—to return extremely attractive and luminous in their original identity, to us, apprentices of their heroism, their commitment, their exemplary militancy. They were the vanguard of the vanguard.

To be a *militante* of the *Frente Sandinista* today is a privilege, the privilege of being the same sort of *militante* as they were. It isn't the privilege of those who inherit an agricultural estate or a business firm or an illustrious surname, but the privilege of modesty, of dignity, of audaciousness, of discipline, of sacrifice.

THE PRIVILEGE OF SELFLESSNESS

Sacrifice is obligation, readiness to forget rest, to postpone the sun and sand of the beach, to renounce the right to violins and the moon, to vacations, to the rocking chair in the doorway of the house. Sacrifice means working without consulting the clock. Sacrifice means war against bad habits, against selfishness.

The privilege I speak of is the privilege of selflessness and unbounded commitment to the interests of the nation, to the resurrection of the oppressed, to die for the nation and the revolution. . . . Dying for country and revolution isn't a sacrifice: it's the greatest of privileges.

Sandino said: "We will go toward the sun of liberty or toward death, and if we die, others will follow us." He knew that death is a bold and agile colt upon which all revolutionaries ride. It isn't suicide—no revolutionary is suicidal. Sandino loved life, loved the rivers, the trees, the nimble hands of his people. That is why he affirmed that "if we die, others will follow us," expressing his unshakable faith in the people, in the oppressed, from whose innermost depths he emerged to defend the dignity and sovereignty of the nation. Sandino had the faith of the prophets, the faith that someday he'd be reborn. And he has been reborn, under numerous pseudonyms: he's been called Rigoberto, Germán, Eduardo, Camilo, Julio, Pedro, Roberto; he's been called Carlos Fonseca, without ceasing to be called Augusto Sandino.

Readiness to die for the country and the revolution impels us to live each moment in joy, to live a life of faith, happiness, and joy in the light of dawn.

THE MEANING OF MILITANCY

The revolutionary's life is water turned into wine, a beautiful experience renewed in each moment of passion and tenderness, in the sharing of clothing without feeling the resultant cold. It's the vocation of risk, of faithfulness to the hymn, the flag, the country. The life of a Nicaraguan revolutionary is one of limitless loyalty to the *Frente Sandinista de Liberación Nacional;* to the *Frente Sandinista* whose founder was Carlos Fonseca, a friend and teacher who combined patriotism with revolutionary theory, whose eyes, piercing the macro and micro cosmos, radiated love and authority. . . .

To be a *militante* is to think of the poor and humble, of the oppressed, twenty-four hours a day, because they are the ones for whom the *Frente* was formed. Our greatest honor is to be *militantes,* living simply and austerely, safeguarding our resources and our reserves with watchful eyes; it is to repudiate the arrogance that demeans and humiliates the one who exercises it, just as it does the one who is subjected to it; to be steadfast in the face of the threats of our enemies. To receive this membership card we've received today entails being like Sandino, like Carlos.

All Nicaraguans have the right and the opportunity to be *militantes* of the Frente Sandinista, but this right has to be conquered with courage, selflessness, and audacity, as one conquers a machinegun nest. The right to be a Sandinista *militante* is won through work—in the militias, in the popular organizations; it is won by modesty and friendship, by overcoming our limitations and errors. Those who are corrupt, cowardly, or opportunistic; the faint-hearted, the hypocritical, the conceited; those who are incapable of dreaming with the future, of crying for a child who dies or of laughing with a child that sings; those who have the soul of a slave, those who've sold their souls to the devil and to imperialism, those who are incapable of loving—all these can never be *militantes* of the *Frente Sandinista de Liberación Nacional.*

The best workers, the best students, the best priests, the best combatants, the best militia members, the most self-denying activists of the popular organizations, the most efficient and selfless functionaries; those businesspersons who are able to renounce the golden calf; those who have the valor to destroy themselves in order to rebuild themselves; those who love, who are deeply moved, who appreciate flowers because flowers make human beings happy; those who are generous, audacious, valiant; those who are ready to suffer and spill their blood for the people—all these have every right to become *militantes* of the *Frente Sandinista de Liberación Nacional.*

Being a *militante* of the *Frente* entails heavy responsibilities. The *militante* is prudent in strategy and audacious in tactics. *Militantes* are leaders and not masters; they place themselves at the front of the people—but not above the people—to guide the people by their examples and sense of direction. They are leaders of conscientious human beings and not of sheep; they earn the right to be heard and respected by self-denial and by the power of example, by being at the vanguard in the hour of sacrifice, of work, and of combat. To Sandinistas the people is and should be as the fire of the gods; as vital as air, water, and food. For Sandinistas the people is root and branch, beginning and end.

BOUNDLESS LOYALTY TO THE PEOPLE

And if Sandinistas are in the vanguard in everything dangerous and demanding, they are in the rear guard at the hour of the awarding of honors—Sandinista audacity in combat and Sandinista reticence in being recognized. We are not, of course, enemies of recognition; we must be fair and generous in recognizing those who never sought recognition for their work and sacrifice. The distribution of membership cards, and today's citations, are an acknowledgment. The *compañeros* have received them with exemplary revolutionary modesty, and those who will later receive them will do so with equal modesty, and would not exchange them for any earthly riches. . . .

For what price would you sell your membership card, Fernando Cardenal? Would you exchange it for the Nobel Peace Prize?[1] I know you deserve it more than anyone else and that it would only be fitting that it be awarded you, but I know very well you wouldn't trade in your Sandinista membership card for this prize or for all the prizes in the world, because your card has no price, because we Sandinistas have no price. No one can buy us, no one can make us surrender, for our treasure is in our revolutionary consciousness, in boundless loyalty to the people. . . .

When we set forth this image of the *militante,* it is not because we are romantic or deluded. Some may think it impossible to forge a new Nicaraguan morality. There were those who likewise thought it would be impossible to assault the *somocista* hell in order to reach paradise; and the Nicaraguan people, with the Sandinistas at its head, achieved that objective. It was difficult, just as it will be difficult to harness the energy of rivers, to link our two great lakes and transform them into crystalline vessels, to build factories and universities, to transform the yellow skin of malnutrition into the fresh skin of healthy persons.

It will be difficult to multiply the loaves in the desert of destruction and disorder, to convert Managua and all our cities into gardens of flowers and fruit; to restore the smell of earth and pastures; to sow the furrows, harvest the sweat of our workers. It is difficult—extremely difficult—to take on the challenge of development and abundance, but we will achieve it, because there isn't anything a revolutionary people cannot achieve.

A STRUGGLE BETWEEN HATE AND LOVE

If it is difficult to rebuild a country, it is even more difficult to rebuild human beings. Human beings are products of their circumstances. Our circumstances have been those of a society in decadence, a society of exploitation and misery, a society of backwardness, of masters and slaves. But there is now a revolution, and that is a new circumstance.

There is in each of us an ongoing struggle between the values of the society we wish to destroy and the values of the society we wish to build: a ceaseless struggle between selfishness and generosity, between individualism and solidarity, between extravagance and austerity, between hate and love. A ferocious struggle from which we will emerge victorious by working out answers to this relentless conflict in every Sandinista conscience. And this struggle is not only personal but social. . . . Our entire society needs to grow politically and ideologically every day, developing its revolutionary morality. Only then will the dawn, positively and forever, have ceased to be a mere enticement.

The *vendepatria* bourgeoisie [who would "sell their homeland"] and imperialism have been overthrown in Nicaragua, but they are struggling to survive. We need to be alert, with our guard up, vigilant and suspicious. For though they no longer hold power, they are resisting like fierce beasts at bay, and are attacking us by making brutal and ruthless use of falsehood to confuse the people, using the press and radio like artillery to vomit their old and rotting ideas upon us, trying to blackmail us economically, threatening to take the little we have from us in order to bring us to our knees. . . .

They try to convince us that the people cannot be master of its own destiny. They say our democracy is totalitarianism, that international solidarity is foreign intervention. They want to rob us of our right to be Nicaraguans, to be Sandinistas, to be patriots, to be in solidarity with the peoples of Latin America. This struggle will be long, difficult, and violent, and can end only with the destruction of the old society, with the victory of revolution.

THE MOST POWERFUL WEAPONS

And what will the most powerful weapons of the revolutionaries be? The example each Sandinista *militante* gives our people: the example of being first in raising production, first in rescuing national values, first in building a new lifestyle and attitude in communion with the masses; of being first in combative readiness, first in solidarity, first in work and last in rest; of being the most efficient in public administration, the most studious, the most convinced that science, art, and technology belong to the people; of being first in understanding that the *Frente Sandinista* is not a club, not an elite; that it isn't a group of favored individuals, but rather of simple, common, and ordinary human beings whose only mark of distinction is their self-denial, modesty, and love for fellow human beings.

It is not enough to reply every day to the lies of reactionaries; it is imperative that we build a new popular and revolutionary morality by our daily example among the people. Without delay we must undertake the resurrection of the truth, so often hidden in the ruins of a society that—sustained by the lies accumulated over the centuries—refuses to die.

Each Nicaraguan is a truth that can be rescued only by the revolution; only in this way can we fulfill our role of vanguard, because the vanguard, *compañeros,* is not an abstraction. The vanguard has a face, bones, blood, and conscience. The vanguard are the men and women who headed the struggle of a heroic people, and who rather than resign themselves to being protagonists of heroism, instead become conscious of their enormous responsibility to reform themselves in order to reform society; a vanguard whose *militantes* take on the qualities of our founders, Carlos Fonseca and Silvio Mayorga[2]—revolutionaries who realize that militancy is won, maintained, or lost, and that it depends on each of us, on our capacity to grow, our capacity to be just, our capacity to love; on our capacity to be true children of that man [Sandino] who sacrificed himself forty-seven years ago, that man who founded the Army for the Defense of National Sovereignty, that man who when asked to lay down his weapons replied in his simple voice of worker and prophet: "I do not surrender. I want a free homeland or death."

OUR SAINTS

Sandino said to the enemies of our people:"I address myself to you traitors, pamphleteers: place yourselves on your knees as I invoke the sacred names of my brothers who offered their lives for our country." Many years later Leonel Rugama speaks to us, saying: "I'd like to speak with you about our saints, who they were, what they were like."[3] In this way Leonel sought to tell us what

militantes of the *Frente Sandinista* should be like: that they should
be like the saints, that they should be like those who sacrificed
themselves; that they should be like those who never vacillated; that
they should be like Carlos Fonseca, like Silvio Mayorga, like
Rigoberto Cruz, like Casimiro Sotelo, like Julio Buitrago, like
Oscar Turcios, like Ricardo Morales, like Eduardo Contreras, like
Carlos Agüero, like Pedro Arauz, like José Benito Escobar. To
them we hand over the fullness of recognition; for them we bow our
heads with profound respect.

NOTES

1. Fernando Cardenal, S.J., coordinated the March-August 1980 National Literacy Crusade, which reduced illiteracy from 50% to 13%, for
which he was nominated for a Nobel Peace Prize. He is today minister of
education. Though he has never formally been asked to renounce his
FSLN membership, the Vatican in August 1984 directed him to abandon
his government post. When he declined to do so, he was expelled from the
Society of Jesus, on December 4, 1984. He continues to be a priest, though
he is barred from administering the sacraments. Cardenal's persistent
commitment to the revolutionary process contrasts with that of the other
militante of whom Borge asked the same question that day: Edén Pastora
was to leave Nicaragua—and the FSLN—within five months, on July 7,
1981.

2. In keeping with revolutionary modesty, Borge makes no mention of
the third founder: himself.

3. Leonel Rugama was a young Christian poet and one of three FSLN
militantes killed in January 1970 in a defiant stand against hundreds of
Somoza's National Guardsmen, who attacked, with tanks and helicopters,
the house where they were staying.

6

On Moral Reconstruction
(1981)

In February 1981, a group of fifty priests, nuns, and lay persons in Nicaragua gathered to reflect on the revolutionary process from a Christian viewpoint. They sought to set forth "a critical perspective as an expression of Christian faithfulness toward the Nicaraguan revolutionary process, grounded in faithfulness to God and the poor, who are the absolute basis of our commitment and perspective." Their discussions gave rise to a document that was published in El Nuevo Diario, *an independent prorevolutionary daily newspaper, on March 24. Following two more months of discussion in Christian base communities, six representatives of these communities were brought together with six Sandinista officials on May 26 for a public dialogue at the Jesuit-run University of Central America (UCA) in Managua. Tomás Borge was among the Sandinista participants.*

This selection is particularly interesting for the insight it affords into the interplay between Sandinism and liberation theology in Nicaragua. Such opponents of the revolution as Cardinal Miguel Obando y Bravo of Managua and Auxiliary Bishop Bosco Vivas have denounced what they disparagingly call "the popular church" as a pliant tool of the Sandinistas. Yet the revolutionary Christians' March 24 document states:

From the best of our Christian faith, we believe the greatest danger for every revolutionary party, and therefore also for the FSLN, is to fall into an exaggerated pride in its own merits and into an attitude of always knowing better than the popular classes what it is they need. . . . In the absence of revolutionary humility, the objectivity needed to analyze situations and understand important problems in depth through the (sometimes ambiguous) signs that emerge from the masses is not favored.[1]

As a case in point, the document analyzes Sandinista policy toward the black and indigenous peoples of the Caribbean littoral of the country. After praising efforts to extend literacy, health care, and communications to the area, the document cautions the Sandinistas that only by humbly listening to the inhabitants of the region can it serve as their revolutionary vanguard.[2] This criticism was made before the Sandinistas changed their Caribbean coast policy, first by curbing military violations of human rights, and later by initiating an Autonomy Process whose methodology included direct consultation (through door-to-door surveys and community meetings) with the inhabitants of the region.

The themes in the document were further elaborated in presentations by representatives of Christian base communities at the UCA conference. Excerpts from two of these are supplied here to give the reader a feel for the quality of the dialogue and to provide context for Borge's response.

FREDDY ROSTRAN
CORRESPONDENT, *RADIO NOTICIAS*

Compañeros, we Christians are both with and within the revolution, and for that very reason we also have a right to be critical of the revolution. The Christian path is "the preferential option for the poor." And that option leads me to press for greater popular participation and communication in government. . . . The leadership of the revolution, represented by the Junta of National Reconstruction, every week engages in dialogue with the people in its "Facing the People" television program. But we don't see this in other strata of the state apparatus. Instead, citizens find themselves facing insurmountable barriers when they try to set forth their problems. . . .

We believe there's a need to contain the exaggerated tendency toward giantism in the state apparatus, and that this must be done through popular participation in the structures of the state. . . .

I repeat: we Christians are with and within the revolution. Every Christian needs to take part in the social transformations underway in Nicaragua, but must also be vigilant concerning errors, abuses, and failings. We must be on the lookout for ostentation among the leaders of our revolution. We must combat bureaucracy in the structures of the state and even in the military structures. Despite all the appeals that have been made, we see the continuing growth of *burocratismo,* of bureaucratic attitudes. And let's not forget that *burocratismo* signifies separation from the people, and most especially from the poor. Finally, we believe that by setting these matters forth as is our right as Christians and Sandinistas, we are defending the revolution. . . .

MARÍA DEL SOCORRO BARRETO
MEMBER, CHRISTIANS IN THE REVOLUTION

The Sandinista Front was the vanguard and guide of the Nicaraguan people in the liberation struggle that brought an end to a corrupt system and began the construction of a new model of society.

We Christians, who believe in Jesus and his message of love, have the obligation to translate this love into service to those who have been marginalized, to those least favored. This commitment has much in common with the principles of the Sandinista Popular Revolution, which has proclaimed itself a revolution for workers and peasants, toward whom it has channeled the major part of its available efforts and resources. This is why many of us Christians, motivated by our faith, have immersed ourselves in the revolution, supporting the revolution and its vanguard, in the confidence that just as it knew how to lead us in the difficult moments of the armed struggle, it would also know how to lead in this new stage of construction of a just, familial, and egalitarian society, always in a spirit of dialogue and of listening to the people.

During the long years of guerrilla insurgency, the FSLN experienced the difficult living conditions of the lower classes. This convivial solidarity with the poor, intimately sharing the austerity of their lives, their sufferings and sacrifices, enabled it to gather and interpret their aspiration as its own. Now, in the stage following the [July 1979] triumph, the leadership of the *Frente,* for reasons of security, has had to undergo a transition from a clandestine lifestyle to a new one that requires another type of housing, of transportation (in cars with opaque windows), and with security checks at offices. To what extent does all this affect and limit direct contact with the people, [blocking] a grasp of the realities of the life of the people? . . .

There is, at the grass roots, a sense that the revolutionary leadership shows great understanding of their problems. Yet Nicaraguans aren't getting the same response from some intermediate sectors, which instead abuse authority and act irresponsibly. Is the National Directorate conscious of this situation? What measures is it taking?

TOMÁS BORGE

Perhaps I should begin by saying that some of the things that have been pointed to here—I'd almost dare say most of the things that have been pointed to—are true.

It was said that the Sandinista Front should be the vanguard of the poor. The Sandinista Front could not be the vanguard if it had not relied on the poor. This must be our point of departure. There was talk of *prepotencia,* of abuse of authority. In the document we are commenting about there is talk of pride, of "heroic pride," and of humility.

We once said that the reconstruction of Nicaragua is a top priority—not the reconstruction of destroyed buildings, not reconstructing factories and hospitals, but reconstructing human life. I think it has perhaps not been sufficiently emphasized that the principal task of the revolution is the moral reconstruction of Nicaragua. For beyond the legacy of physical destruction we also have the terrible legacy of moral destruction.

There was talk here of bureaucracy. I have to confess that bureaucracy is becoming a straitjacket hampering the revolution. There was talk of *prepotencia,* of the abuse of power. And we must confess that there is such abuse among many government officials, and particularly in the armed forces.

I must confess that there isn't enough austerity on the part of government officials. We must make the utmost effort not only to be the vanguard of the poor but also to integrate ourselves with the poor. Recently in the National Directorate we were discussing what we might do to live more closely with the poor. And the majority of the *compañeros* agreed that we should live in the barrios of Managua. However, someone pointed out that if we were to go live in the barrios of Managua, necessary security measures would compel us to live in a different manner from that of the people who live there. We couldn't, for example, go around on bicycles; for security reasons we must use motor vehicles. There would be too striking a contrast between our physical presence there and the way of life of the poor population in the barrios. We thought the remedy in this case was even worse than the illness.

I think we need to combat bureaucracy in the manner indicated by *compañero* Emilio [Baltodano]: through the people, through the mass organizations. But public officials should also become conscious of what *burocratismo* signifies in this country. We have seen truly dramatic and at time ridiculous examples of *burocratismo*. I know of the example of a *compañera* who was seven months pregnant. And when she came to request a certificate of pregnancy at an institution here, she was told to return with proof of pregnancy. If you don't call that *burocratismo,* I don't know what to call *burocratismo*. And I could say much more about *burocratismo,* and likewise about arrogance, about the lack of humility.

And another important thing: it has been said here that there should be close contact between the leaders of the revolution and the people. Yes, it seems to me that at times we have fallen into a merely formal contact with the masses. It comes down to those "Facing the People" programs—which, let me say in passing, have been excellent and very well managed. But many of the responses given there cannot be complete, because the television cameras are in the middle of it all and we have to be very cautious. Perhaps a more direct approach would be better, with the leaders of the revolution meeting with workers, going to the barrios. If we cannot allow ourselves the luxury and the immense satisfaction of living among them, at least we could learn something by spending a day or two with workers in the barrios. I think some *compañeros* have done this.

What's more, criticism directed at the intermediate cadres of the *Frente* should be addressed to us instead. I believe that as leaders we are obligated to maintain an intimate contact with the masses, a much closer contact. And the intermediate cadres generally do what the most prominent leaders of a revolution do. And the day we leave our offices (because we have had to spend much time in our offices in order to form the new revolutionary state) to go to the barrios and the work places, we will advance. The National Directorate, which is very wise in these matters, has already decided to do so.[3] In fact, this very afternoon we have just come from speaking with the workers of Texaco.

I believe that many of the Christian virtues are valid for all revolutionaries, whether or not they be Christians. I have profound respect for the moral virtues of Christianity. In fact, I have personally discovered that the practice of certain Christian virtues brings tremendous joy to the human spirit.

We should be humble. This is a magnificent Christian virtue that should be practiced by revolutionaries. We should, for example, engage in revolutionary criticism. Christians speak of confession, and there is a correspondence between criticism and confession. I believe that criticism is a special form of confession and that we should practice it every day and every moment. We should be permanent targets of criticism, because the leaders of a revolution should be, as we have at times said, a kind of showcase under the critical gaze of all the people, and subject to the revolutionary vigilance of all the people.

There has also been talk of faithfulness. I think that Christians, to be faithful to their Christian principles, have to begin by being faithful to their nation. Self-proclaimed Christians who are unfaithful to their nation aren't true Christians, in my judgment. Those who don't practice Christianity, true Christianity, can't be on the side of their nation, because they are loyal to interests foreign to Nicaragua.

We should interweave humility with respect for national dignity. We have just come from speaking with the workers of Texaco . . . [and] the manager there didn't want to allow the workers to meet on the premises. And when he was informed that we were to participate in the event, he said: "the *comandantes de la revolución* are worth shit." Well, then, we must be humble; we are humble. I think we should be so with the poor, with the workers. But with these elements, betrayers of their homeland (and what's more the fellow is Nicaraguan), we should be proud, we should be very dignified. "Tomorrow," we said, "because of the respect that should be accorded our revolution, this individual should be called before the police to answer for the things he said in front of the workers."

Christians have said they are with the revolution. I can assure them that the revolution is also with the Christians—to the extent that just about everything that has so far been brought up seems absolutely right to me.[4]

On occasion I would speak with Father Molina, our great friend and brother, and say to him: it won't be possible to fulfill the task of the Sandinistas without the participation of Christians. And I believe a true integration should be formed between Christians and Sandinistas—not merely a tactical unity, or even a strategic one, but a true integration to carry forward this revolutionary process, and to reconstruct the most important thing in need of reconstruction here, which is the moral formation of human life in Nicaragua.

NOTES

1. *Los cristianos interpelan a la revolución: fidelidad crítica en el proceso de Nicaragua* (Managua: Coedición IHCA-CAV, 1981), p. 30.

2. *Ibid.,* p. 31.

3. Borge makes frequent *recorridos,* walking tours, of barrios throughout the country, engaging in face-to-face discussion with residents and passersby.

4. This paragraph has been relocated from its original position in order to improve organization and readability.

7

Law and Social Justice
(1981)

In a 1983 address to a theological conference in Madrid (p. 116) Borge characterized the Frente Sandinista *as antidogmatic, a quality not readily associated with Marxist governing parties. Indeed, FSLN openness and flexibility, so evident in its ground-breaking relationship with Christians, is a manifestation of its creative adaptation of Marxist methodology to its Sandinista heritage. This relationship between Marxist analysis and Sandinista purposes is perhaps nowhere as evident as in this May 23, 1981, address to an audience of national and foreign jurists gathered in Managua for the Silvio Mayorga Juridical Conference.*

In a perceptive analysis co-published by Managua's prorevolution Antonio Valdivieso Ecumenical Center, Italian Marxist theologian Giulio Girardi points out that the Marxisms of contemporary Marxist-Leninist states (most notably the U.S.S.R. with its lingering Stalinist legacy) are primarily deductive, deriving their practices from an a priori law of "dialectical materialism," which sees reality as entirely determined by the interactions of matter. This dogma severely constricts the realm of human freedom, inclining its adherents toward a mechanistic view of history, intolerance of dissent, and militant atheism.[1]

Sandinista Marxism, on the other hand, is primarily inductive, allowing political theory to emerge organically (and in accord with genuine scientific method) from the data of revolutionary practice.

66

It is this empiricism, Girardi argues, that has enabled the FSLN to design new Marxist concepts of democracy, human rights, and religion out of its Nicaraguan experience.

Furthermore, inasmuch as the Sandinistas have availed them-selves of "historical materialism" (the inductive, scientific analysis of history) without also adopting the metaphysical dogma of "dialectical materialism," the question of end-values remains open. It is here that Borge reinforces the profoundly humane legacy of Sandino and Fonseca by committing Marxist tools of social trans-formation to explicitly moral purposes, among them the transfor-mation of human beings and nations from objects to subjects of history, and the profound respect for human life and conscience in which that quest is rooted.

It is noteworthy that Borge finds certain Christian concepts especially fitting to define these Sandinista moral purposes. This is underscored when, after admitting to a nonreligious gathering that he's received a lot of criticism for his oft-repeated statement that the revolution is not out to eliminate sinners but their sins, he undauntedly proceeds to tell them that Nicaraguans need to learn to love their enemies. And when he quotes Peruvian Marxist José Carlos Mariátegui to the effect that "we are fighting for beauty as well as bread," the connection with Jesus' "human beings do not live by bread alone" is inescapable in the Latin American context, where moral virtue is a particularly esteemed form of beauty.

I was, as some of you know, a law student at the university [in León]. There we were presented with the image of law as an absolute science, as an independent and immutable phenomenon in human society. We were told that law is the accumulation of knowledge that is continually being perfected by humankind. We were told that there are no bad laws, only bad judges, and that there are no connections between law and politics. Law and justice, the professors told us, are one and the same; they are universal, transcending time and space.

As to the coexistence of exploiters and exploited, the professors' attitude was one of resignation. The tyrant [Anastasio Somoza García] and his cronies spoke to us of peace, and to our amazement these scholarly mouths repeated such preachments of civic duty and opposition to violence while the finest of our people were being beaten, tortured, and murdered.

Our national heroes were treated as delinquents, when they weren't entombed in anonymity; and the true delinquents were granted high-sounding titles. You will recall how Somoza was referred to as "the peacemaker," as "champion of democracy."

Professors and periodicals made everyday use of the word "democracy," and when in amazement we would ask, "and this is democracy?," explanations abounded to excuse the "inevitable faults and imperfections." It isn't difficult to deduce the effect all these fallacious and unscientific conceptions had on the legal profession and the implementation of justice.

THE BEST TEACHER

Revolutionary practice, which is the best teacher, taught us in the exacting school of social confrontation that it is impossible to separate the judicial system from the character of the state; that law is a conjunction of norms sanctioned by the state, and that these norms are shaped and colored by the interests that control the state apparatus. Reality taught us that in the society in which we lived—and live—some persons exploited others; that human beings were—and are—divided by the material conditions of their existence.

We had barely learned the use of the guerrilla's rifle when contact with the dispossessed masses taught us that the great landholder, the powerful banker, and the high-ranking military officer were not wax figures but human beings of flesh and blood and tooth and nail, cruel possessors of wealth and political power; that they were the beneficiaries of laws expressly framed to favor their interests; and that the industrial worker, the poor peasant, and the artisan were subject to laws purposely framed to crush them. The revolutionary struggle taught us that the values of the great landholder aren't the same as the values of the humble peasant.

The revolutionary struggle taught us that in the mouths of traditional politicians, peace and civic duty were but public relations gimmicks, mere propaganda, and that it was utopian to expect wealthy egotists to become generous and voluntarily give up their privileges.

The revolutionary struggle taught us the need to dispose of the false images of our Latin American heroes—the lies and justifications manufactured by the ruling classes in order to oppress us; that it was a fundamental historical obligation of revolutionaries to remove our heroes from their tombs, to uncover their true light—their word and their example—with profound respect; and that only revolutionaries could identify the essence of heroism. Fray Bartolomé de Las Casas, Bolívar, Martí, and Sandino have at last emerged unscathed from the filthy, demagogic oratory with which they had been trampled in anniversary celebrations.[2]

We learned through all the stages of the revolutionary struggle that a revolution that loses its vocation of defense ceases to be a revolution; that to defend our land razed by foreign intervention, by pillage and destruction, our tiny republic, impoverished but today enriched by the joy of newfound freedom, would have to be armed with patriotism and rifles, even though we are not military types.[3] For we know that in the jungles of Latin American anti-democracy, trained brutes only await the signals of their masters to bare their fangs and sink them in our peoples' entrails.

Our revolutionary struggle taught us that a revolution that fears the people, that distrusts the people, is not a revolution; that revolution is the people; that the people is the revolution; that revolutionary leadership is not something you can buy at the corner store or the supermarket, but requires long years of sacrifice and struggle. It takes years to learn to love the people with all one's heart, to earn the people's belief and respect. . . .

LAW AND POLITICS

So it wasn't the professors of substantive and procedural methods and of civil and criminal law who taught us about the inseparable linkage between law and its political inspiration. Nor was it they who showed us that behind every legal norm lie the interests of the social sector that conceived and enacted it. It was the revolutionary struggle that taught us that every law is a political act, and as such reflects particular material interests; that there is no such thing as justice or law in the abstract, valid for all times and all societies. Justice and law are unconcealable expressions of governing interests. . . .

Civil and mercantile law, which I understand are still in effect, were enacted in order to defend the inherited interests of the bourgeoisie and the landholders. Why, for example, was the August 6, 1937, law of agricultural and industrial collateral put into effect? In practice it was used to protect usury and to guarantee timely payments of interest. It was logical: who, among others, were in power? Usurers, powerful merchants. The law of August 6, 1937, was obviously a political law.

On April 4, 1929, *La Gaceta* [the official government journal] published the agreement between the governments of the United States and Nicaragua by which the National Guard was founded. The regulations for the government and discipline of the National Guard were published that same year, and were followed in 1934 by the code of military justice. These laws were badly translated copies of U.S. army regulations, which continued to be in effect long after they were repealed in the United States. In fact, it was by these laws that we Sandinistas, in court-martial, were judged and sentenced. The current president of the Supreme Court of Justice, Dr. Roberto Argüello Hurtado, was one of our principal and bravest defenders on that occasion. Dr. Rafael Córdoba Rivas likewise distinguished himself by his courage in defending numerous Sandinistas at that difficult time.[4] These were the same laws by which [William] Walker executed Nicaraguan patriots in 1856, and by which collaborators of [Sandino's] Army in Defense of National Sovereignty were judged.[5] These laws inherited from foreign occupation were—who could doubt it?—political acts.

The military laws now in force form an organic unity that guides the conduct of the Sandinista Armed Forces. These very strict laws go well beyond ordinary legislation. Typical examples include the prohibition of maltreatment of prisoners—the law speaks of abuse in either word or deed—and the obligation to treat the sick and wounded. The new military laws, which are extremely tough and at the same time profoundly humane, reflect with maturity and seriousness the confidence the Nicaraguan people has placed in the new revolutionary state. The military laws of the revolution are likewise political acts.

LAW IN THE SOMOZA ERA

Despite the fact that our laws were fashioned to satisfy the selfishness of exploiters prior to and during the Somoza era, *somo-*

cista corruption became so extreme that not even the very laws that guaranteed the interests of the dominant classes were respected. For the dominant classes had a flair for incest; they had no trouble violating the laws that were their own daughters, when they no longer served to defend their interests. Judges and magistrates were loyal members of Ali Baba's gang. The most powerful politicians of the Somoza era sold their influence in the supreme court and courts of appeal like luxury items.

To point out just one aspect of the corruption and brutal character of the laws in past regimes, more than 80 percent of civil judgments were court-ordered seizures [of collateralized property]. . . . Preventive attachment was, as the lawyers here well remember, the juridical form used to legalize armed plunder directed by a judge, a judge who was usually pot-bellied and invariably devoid of human sentiment. The professional fees for the execution of the seizure were drawn from the debtor's goods. Poor debtor! There were corporations specially set up as collection agencies to engage in legalized pillage.

Justice and law, as has often been repeated here, had their price. In agrarian and industrial proceedings landholders and capitalists had not only the advantage of laws that favored them but also the further advantage that the worker and peasant couldn't afford to compete for merchandise in the supermarket of judicial verdicts. Who could compete with men like Cornelio Hueck, Granera Padilla, and so many other representatives of the Somoza regime?

JUSTICE: BLIND, BUT NOT DEAF

Justice has traditionally been symbolized by a blindfolded woman holding aloft a balance, by which we've been made to believe that justice is blind—meaning, it is impartial in applying the law. Yet our people, who suffered this kind of justice, was able to say, with an element of retributive humor, that justice is blind but not deaf, because she always inclined the balance toward the loudest sound of clanging coins; the same clanging of coins that was heard by Judas, the Judas who betrayed the crucified Christ.

During the Somoza era it was virtually a crime to be honest. Do you remember? Whoever did not rob was considered a fool and an idiot (I will refrain from using the actual expression they used). Robbery conferred social distinction, and the more one robbed, the more distinguished, gentlemanly, and illustrious one was. Meanwhile, to be patriotic, anti-imperialist, and revolutionary was to reach the highest extreme of delinquency in our country.

A NEW UNDERSTANDING OF LAW AND JUSTICE

But the death certificate of that corrupt and repressive regime was signed in blood on July 19, [1979]. The dominion of imperialism and its coercive organizations—the National Guard, Somoza's Security Office, the Tribunals of Justice—was buried forever on that historic date. From that moment on we initiated a series of qualitative changes. Our point of departure was a dependent and backward society; our strategic objective was a superior society to be reached by way of a democratic, popular, and anti-imperialist revolution.

We must now form a state organized to ensure the participation of an ever more conscious, wise, and productive people. Political liberation, rooted in the new society, reaches out to smash the shell of the old superstructure and give rise to a new and solid superstructure. The judicial apparatus of today coexists dialectically with that of yesterday, and in the transition to a new state this contradiction will give rise to a new conception of justice and law.

Though human beings have changed in the course of the revolution, such has not been the case with the laws—the bad laws, despite what we were told in the university. Practice has shown us that it is not enough to have good judges when the laws go against the grain of history, of the new reality created by revolution. . . .

THE SOPHISM OF EQUALITY BETWEEN UNEQUALS

So far I've been referring to a particular society: Nicaraguan society. But when we look at human history, the magnitude of human social transformations makes it easy to detect the relationships among law, justice, liberty, and the state.

What justice, what right, and what laws characterized the conduct of human beings in the era of slavery (an era that lasted thousands of years)? In the modern age no one has the legal right to own another human being. Yet possession of other human beings was a right upheld by law in slaveholding societies. The slaveholder could buy, sell, and even kill the slave. Recall the struggles of Spartacus and the brutal repression to which slaves were subjected when they tried to free themselves from slaveholders. And from what were they trying to free themselves? From the laws in force in that period. Slaves were subversives who violated the law.

When peasants worked the land of the master of the sword and the gallows, and were paid in kind or simply received the usufruct of a piece of land, it was in compliance with the law; these relationships among human beings were in conformity with the law imposed by feudal lords and kings. . . .

With the advent of the bourgeois revolution there emerges the sophism of equality before the law, a merely formal equality. For never have capitalists and workers been equal. Who is fooled by the assertion that the owner of a large enterprise has the same rights before the law as do his workers? Agricultural and industrial workers know what the reality is from their own experience. The bourgeoisie discovered the beautiful language of equality, but reality is stubborn about facts. Equality between unequals, between owners and nonowners, is more than a simple sophism: it's a cruel mockery of historical truth. . . .

The point is that the social classes in power impose their own norms. We cannot, if we are to be objective, speak abstractly of justice, rights, and law. There's the justice, rights, and law of the slaveholder against slaves; the justice, rights, and law of the masters of the sword and the gallows against serfs; the justice, rights, and law of the landholders and industrialists against peasants and workers; the justice, rights, and law of exploiters against the exploited—just as there is also the justice, rights, and law of the revolutionary classes against the reactionary classes.

In political struggle the dichotomy between friend and enemy is a false one, because the real contradiction is between exploiter and exploited, between oppressor and oppressed; between those who defend the opulence of a few vis-à-vis the martyrdom of the many, and enjoy the protection of nonexposure to perpetuate exploitation, and those who, armed with light and ammunition, with their words and their blood, build a country of free human beings.

What, for example, was the law of the *somocistas*? To rob others under the shelter of *somocista* legality. What is the law of the revolutionaries? To imprison those who steal from the public treasury. . . .

So yesterday's persecutors are today's persecuted; yesterday's jailers are today's prisoners. But there's a difference. The difference is that yesterday's persecutors were murderers, torturers, human beasts, whereas today's revolutionaries are profoundly humane, respectful of the life and dignity of the human being.

No revolution—no genuine revolution, that is—sets out to humiliate human beings; on the contrary, the fundamental objective has been and is to achieve human dignity, which means rescuing human beings from the humiliation to which they are subjected by the contemporary forms of slavery.

A SHOWCASE OF HUMAN RIGHTS

We once said we would become a showcase of human rights . . . [and] this revolution has been generous beyond what could be required of it. It is the first revolution in human history without firing squads, without tear gas canisters, and with habeas corpus. . . . We are not tempted toward reprisal, or toward arrogance and authoritarianism. Our one temptation, as you know, has been that of making a new day dawn.

I'm going to make a confession, however. Human rights are not completely respected in Nicaragua. There exists the political will to respect them, but as long as there is unemployment, homelessness, barefooted and hungry children, children who die for lack of medical attention; as long as there are landless *campesinos;* as long as there are human beings who live in abundance while others are in misery; as long as there are human beings who laugh while others cry; as long as a woman has to surrender her body in order to feed her children; as long as the hands of children are extended in restaurant entryways for a piece of bread; as long as true equality is but an intention—the human rights of Nicaraguans are not being respected.

Unfortunately, our poor country, fenced in by criminal pressures, half asphyxiated by foreign debt and technological and energy dependency, cannot fully respond to these problems at the moment. For now we limit ourselves to respecting individual human rights as they have never before been respected in our country. Political murder, torture, and even verbal abuse of prisoners have disappeared forever in Nicaragua. That's not to say there can't be isolated exceptions, because this is an ongoing process.

LOVING OUR ENEMIES

Within the context of respect for individual human rights, we have planned a modern and profoundly humane penitentiary system for Nicaragua. . . . To many it may seem strange, but we are moral enough to educate our people about generosity. It may seem strange, but we hold no grudges against ex-National Guardsmen. We wish instead to transform them from human beasts into human beings. That is the design of the revolution. We want these men to have work, to maintain their family ties.

All across the country we have preached that the children of Guardsmen are to be treated the same as children of Sandinistas, and that a child of a murderer of our people is to be valued as much as a child of Carlos Fonseca. We must extend the same love and tenderness to the child of an imprisoned thief or murderer as to the child of [martyred *comandante*] Germán Pomares. This is a plea we make to children when we go to the barrios, because they initially discriminated against the children of Guardsmen, children who are not to blame for the crimes of their fathers. What's more, their fathers were themselves victims of the social system we lived in, and our duty, as we've said before, is not to eliminate the sinners, but to destroy the sin.

I've received a lot of correspondence criticizing me for the way I express myself on this subject. Nevertheless our people has to learn to love its enemies. Our people needs to fill its heart with love for all human beings. The best way to treat prisoners is to educate them and create work opportunities for them. Why don't those who are writing demagogic articles in the newspaper [*La Prensa*] instead put together a carpentry workshop? Let them do something constructive instead of indulging in worthless rhetoric. We, instead of writing articles talking about liberty for the Guardsmen, are endeavoring to truly liberate them from their past, from their crimes, through education.

STRUGGLE FOR BREAD AND BEAUTY

As part of our effort to set an example of respect for human rights, the *Junta de Gobierno,* on August 21, 1979, approved the Statute of Rights and Guarantees of the Nicaraguan People. Three months later we signed the American Convention on Human Rights.

The revolution has taught more than 400,000 persons how to read, has increased the education budget from 330 million cordobas to 1.15 billion cordobas in 1981, and has increased student enrollment from 500,000 to more than 800,000. The budget for health care has risen from 202 million cordobas under Somoza to 1.2 billion cordobas (1981). Unemployment has been reduced from 28 percent to 17 percent, and the revolution intends to eliminate it shortly. Public transportation, water, and electricity are subsidized.

Whereas *somocismo* permitted 174 labor unions, many of which were controlled by the dictatorship, the revolution has conferred juridical status on 307 unions. More unions have been recognized in two years than in all of previous Nicaraguan history. Three hundred collective bargaining agreements have been signed, and miners are protected by such an agreement for the first time. . . .

The Ministry of Culture has created forty-six poetry and dance workshops, some of which are in the army and police. There are ninety amateur theater groups, and we are developing an ever more creative cinema.

This is fighting for human rights, but it is only the beginning. These are the first steps of a people struggling to attain abundance and love, to secure true rights, true justice, true liberty, where human beings are equal before the law and equal in their social relationships. For in the words of Peruvian thinker José Carlos Mariátegui, we struggle not only for bread but for beauty.[6]

HUMAN BEINGS AS CONSCIOUS CREATORS OF HISTORY

We have repeatedly been asked what answer the revolution can provide to the problem of justice, of revolutionary legality. In the first place we'd like to indicate that the legal reforms necessary to establish harmony between the base and the superstructure of society should be discussed by all the people. We do not envision laws of importance to the revolution that do not originate in popular discussion; instead we envision full participation by all the people in discussions of fundamental laws . . . a back-and-forth mechanism between the organized masses and state institutions.

In any event, the new justice should be designed to break with alienation, to bring an end to human beings as objects. Human beings should be the constructors of history, not the puppets of surreptitious forces. We envision a society of conscious human beings, not a society of robots.

We realize that law does not in and of itself bring about a substantial transformation within a social process. . . . Nevertheless, law that doesn't eliminate contradictions but is born of them should be the result of democratic consultation with all the people, and therefore the normative expression of legitimate interests secured by the revolution.

Only revolution opens the real possibility of transforming law into an instrument of change. In this sense law will have to be democratic not only in its execution but also in its design. Legal professionals would be solitary passers-by along the path of justice were not the experience and justice of the people to walk alongside them.

Popular participation will without a doubt be the best antidote to bureaucracy; it will help keep the language of the law comprehensible; it will ensure that no crime lacks its corresponding sanction. We, the forces of revolution, therefore prepare ourselves to fight inflexibility, arcane language, cumbersome proceedings, and casuistic interpretations of the law.

We will unite all our efforts to achieve the goal of a revolutionary legal system: to create laws that are in harmony with reality, that are objective, that are profoundly humane, like adroit sentinels—not like barbarous Attilas—looking out for the tranquility and happiness of the people.[7]

We will declare war on bureaucracy and delinquency, on counterrevolutionary conspiracy and judicial sluggishness. Judges, police, lawyers, workers and peasants, protagonists of the revolution, let's move forward to dislodge the injustice of our land, forward in the conquest of justice and the rights of our people! A free homeland or death!

NOTES

1. Giulio Girardi, *Sandinismo, Marxismo, Cristianismo en la Nueva Nicaragua* (Mexico City: Ediciones Nuevomar, 1986).

2. Fray Bartolomé de Las Casas (1474–1566), bishop of Chiápas (today the southernmost state of Mexico), was a persistent defender of the rights of indigenous peoples in New Spain, and eventually became an opponent of black slavery as well.

Simón Bolívar (1783–1830) was to northern South America what George Washington was to the United States. He liberated five countries from the Spanish empire (Colombia, Ecuador, Peru, Bolivia, and his native Venezuela), and proposed a Latin American confederation as a counterpart to the great Anglo-American federation of the north.

José Martí (1853–1895) was a Cuban poet and founder of the Cuban Revolutionary Party who dedicated his life to achieving independence for his country. He became a martyr when he was murdered by the Spanish occupation forces upon his return from exile.

3. Borge here echoes Augusto Sandino, who in 1933 told journalist Ramón de Belausteguigoitia: "As you can see, we are not military types. We are of the people, we are armed citizens!" (Sergio Ramírez, ed., *Augusto C. Sandino: El Pensamiento Vivo* [Managua: Editorial Nueva Nicaragua, 1984], vol. 2, p. 293.

4. Rafael Córdova Rivas is a leader of the Democratic Conservative Party (PCD), and was then one of three members of the governing *Junta de Reconstrucción Nacional,* serving alongside Daniel Ortega and Sergio Ramírez. He was elected to the National Assembly on the PCD slate in November 1984, where he has since distinguished himself on the Constitutional Commission.

5. After landing in Nicaragua with a force of U.S. freebooters in 1855, Tennesseean William Walker took possession of the country and used it as a base for his intended conquest of all Central America, by which he intended to add five more slave states (and ten senators) to the Union. By 1857 he was defeated and executed in Honduras, though not before leaving a trail of blood across the Nicaraguan landscape.

6. José Carlos Mariátegui was a Peruvian Marxist essayist whose unorthodox, distinctively Latin American, views distanced him from the Communist International Party. His writings are among Borge's favorites.

7. The inscription over the entryway to the headquarters of the Ministry of the Interior in downtown Managua *(Edificio Silvio Mayorga)* reads: "Ministry of the Interior, Sentinel of the People's Happiness."

8

The Christianity That Follows Christ and the Christianity That Uses Christ (1982)

This selection consists of responses to questions asked by partici-
pants at the Conference of Religious Organizations of Central and
South America held in Managua in 1982.

Of special interest is Borge's opening statement that he is a
Christian, reaffirmed at the conclusion. This is the first time a
leader of a Marxist-Leninist vanguard party has pronounced him-
self a Christian. Although his definition of what it means to be a
Christian will hardly satisfy conservatives looking for a Johannine
statement of belief in the metaphysical deity of Jesus, it compares
most favorably with Jesus' own Great Commandment.

Borge reveals even more about his understanding of discipleship
in the tribute he pays to Archbishop Oscar Romero, describing him
as a Latin American apostle. Against this model, he contrasts the
religious frauds being perpetrated against the church by Nicara-
guan counterrevolutionaries intent on manipulating religious sym-
bols for their political ends.

What does it mean to be a Christian? I am no expert in theology
or in religious matters, but if being a Christian is to be good, if
being Christian is to be honest, if being Christian is to have profound respect for others, if being Christian is to fill one's soul and

heart with love for others, I am a Christian [applause]. . . .

Conversing recently with a Maryknoll sister who is not only a woman but an angel—her name is Peggy [Healy]—I said to her: "how can it be (because she is very physically attractive) that you've renounced all the satisfactions of common and ordinary human beings, that you've left your homeland, that you've renounced marriage and maternity even though you're still young and attractive?"

She then said something that moved me deeply: "No, I'm not making any sacrifice at all. I'm not making any sacrifice, because what I'm doing fills me with satisfaction, so that I feel fully realized." It is these genuinely revolutionary and internationalist religious missionaries who have been expelled from this country, but not by the revolutionary power.[1]

For the first time an opportunity has emerged for integral collaboration between a revolution that has attained power and the [institutional] church, but the vanity and attachment to class interests of some religious figures, and their fear of socialism, lead them to scorn this possibility. There is also an escalation of fear in some sectors of the upper hierarchy of the Latin American church, because the sort of alliance or integration that emerges between Christians and the revolution in Nicaragua has implications for all of Latin America. And because imperialism is worried about the very existence of this revolution, there are also some who are worried about this integration, this beautiful integration between Christian principles and revolutionary principles.

Religious freedom is one of the components of liberty that we believe must be inflexibly maintained. We have said before and we repeat now that as long as there is revolution in our country, there will be religious freedom—that is to say, always, because there will always be revolution in this country [applause].

OSCAR ROMERO, MARTYR OF LATIN AMERICA

What shall I say about Archbishop Romero? In the case of certain persons, it is sometimes more eloquent to be silent; because, beyond being a bishop, Oscar Romero was an apostle. I daresay the blood of this man was not spilled only in El Salvador but throughout Latin America, and from his wounds flowed the blood of all who have fallen on this continent, and moreover the blood that continues to flow from the sacrifices of all who die for their ideals. And to think that there are those who see the same vestments and are incapable of feeling the infinite tenderness and self-denial that Oscar Romero felt for his people!

A banner with portrait of Archbishop Oscar Romero hangs from the cathedral in Estelí: "Faithful, steadfast, and heroic."

"Oscar Romero was more than a bishop; he was an apostle."

Will he have a repercussion in Latin America? He already has. Someday, when we take measure of our heroes and when history gathers the names of those who have contributed most through their sacrifices and struggles, it will be necessary to identify Archbishop Romero among the first of them. This Christian and revolutionary, this exceptional human being, had the additional virtue of being humble and unpretentious. God grant that all priests, all

Christians, and all revolutionaries might at the very least learn from Oscar Romero's humility, a virtue not found in abundance in some other ecclesiastical figures. Archbishop Romero is Salvadoran and is of you and is of all of us [applause].

MANIPULATING RELIGIOUS SENTIMENTS

A struggle has been fomented in the heart of the Christian communities in Nicaragua. Some have sought to manipulate the religious sentiments of our people, and it disturbs us deeply that this manipulation is, above all, an act of disrespect for the sentiments of our people. Because in the name of religious freedom and the power of Christianity, some falsehoods have been invented, some supposed miracles that we know are not miracles, because we've been very careful in our investigations. For example, it was discovered that the person who proclaimed the "miracle" of the sweating virgin was a dissembler, and we are accumulating proof regarding other apparitions that have been claimed around here. Supposing for a moment that the miracle was genuine, we would truly be scoundrels if we were to want to suppress it when it seems to have all the traits of a genuine miracle, even though it cannot be proved (because this is very difficult). But if we have evidence that this is instead a hoax, who and what are these scoundrels showing disrespect for? The Christian people and the symbols of Christianity.

Hasn't the Virgin Mary been the object of veneration by this people? Every year on the seventh of December [*La Purísima*], Nicaraguans walk the streets, crying out: "Who brings such happiness?" They then respond: "The conception of Mary!" In the heart of all Nicaraguan Christians the Virgin is the Mother of God—of Jesus Christ—who was a woman of exceptional qualities, and she's been held in great honor. And when hoaxes of this kind are fabricated, who is shown disrespect? Is it not this woman who symbolizes Christian purity, who is venerated by the Nicaraguan people? One would have to be a real villain to spit in the face of this woman who represents purity in Christianity, and one would have to be perverse to insult, spit upon, and trample underfoot the religious sentiments of our people. This is what we do not pardon. They also manipulate religious symbols against the revolution, because they say the Virgin appeared on account of the arrival of communism, that the Virgin appeared to save Nicaragua. But it isn't this that bothers us so much as the lack of respect for our Christian people and their religious symbols.

USING CHRIST AGAINST THE REVOLUTION

When I said "Sandino yesterday, Sandino today, Sandino forever," and afterward this was converted into a slogan, into a revolutionary motto, I wasn't thinking of Christ, I was thinking of Sandino. Some others later came up with "Christ yesterday, Christ today, Christ forever," something said by Saint Paul [Heb. 13:8, though modern authorities do not ascribe the letter to Paul], but it had never been used here as a popular religious axiom [applause]. Because when they say "Christ yesterday, Christ today, Christ forever," the latter-day pharisees aren't thinking of Christ. They are not doing it to exalt Christ but to attack the revolution.

They say "Christ is coming." I asked one of those priests who are saying that Christ is coming: "And where in the devil did he go?" [laughter and applause]. "Do you suppose he went off to Paraguay? Or that he's been sunning in a bikini on the beaches at Miami? Don't be disrespectful, Christ isn't *going to come,* because Christ is here and is never going to leave" [applause]. . . .

They are using Christ as a counterrevolutionary instrument, using Christ to confound the humble, using Christ to counter the revolution. Yet when Christ came, he didn't go to Plastic City [a U.S.-style shopping plaza in Managua, catering to the well-to-do] or to COSEP [the High Council of Private Enterprise] in search of disciples, but to the seashore in search of fishermen and workers [applause]. They would like to oppose Christ to the revolution, but Christ was a revolutionary [applause]. They'd like to oppose Christ to the poor, but Christ was poor and a friend of the poor [applause]. They'd like to oppose Christ to the humble, but Christ was humble. Never did their counterparts exchange champagne toasts with Christ; never did they invite him to the bosom of the Roman empire as they have invited some who call themselves representatives of Christ to the bosom of Yankee imperialism [applause].[2]

That is why we can say as Sandinistas: "Sandino yesterday, Sandino today, Sandino forever," and as Christians, though not for demagogical reasons or to oppose this motto to the revolutionary motto, "Christ yesterday, Christ today, Christ forever" [applause]. And when Nicaraguans are gathered together in the public squares we can cry out *¡Viva Sandino!* just as we can cry out in church *¡Viva Cristo!* Such is our position.

I say "Christians and Sandinistas": just as Christians can be Sandinistas, so can Sandinistas be Christians. And if I someday manage to become, as I aspire to, a humble being: if I someday manage to become, as I aspire to, a righteous being: if I am able to genuinely set aside my weaknesses; if I should prove capable of joining in fullness with the poor—on that day I will repeat what I have said now, except with greater reason and propriety: I am, like yourselves, a disciple of Christ.

NOTES

1. Cardinal Miguel Obando y Bravo of Managua has removed dozens of priests and nuns from their parishes as a consequence of their support for the revolution. Those of foreign nationality have generally been transferred out of the country. On the other side of the ledger (and very likely in a spirit of quid pro quo), ten foreign priests were expelled from the country on Borge's orders in the summer of 1984, after they had participated in a demonstration of support for Amado Peña, a right-wing priest closely linked to the cardinal, who was filmed on videotape in the process of collaborating with agents of the armed counterrevolution. Peña (a Nicaraguan national) was placed under house arrest and later pardoned.

2. Cardinal Obando y Bravo traveled to Washington in January 1982, where he was honored by the neoconservative Institute for Religion and Democracy, and met with Thomas Enders, assistant secretary of state for Latin American Affairs.

9

The Lake as Mirror of Our Values
(1982)

This speech, delivered on March 27, 1982, in Managua, was the closing address at the Seminar on Saving Lake Managua, held under the auspices of the Nicaraguan Institute for Natural Resources and the Environment (IRENA).

Its contributions are several. Through a case study of Lake Xolotlán (also known as Lake Managua), it provides a view of another, seldom-discussed side of the Somoza dynasty's legacy of death: that of ecological destruction and its human consequences. Going beyond mere technical analysis, Borge probes deeper questions of perception and motivation. The problem, he suggests, is that just as capitalism fails to value human beings for themselves, so does it fail to value nature for itself. In the very measure that it does what it is intended to do—maximize the figure on the bottom line—it cannot see the forest for the square feet of lumber.

Against this model, Borge propounds a Franciscan vision of society founded on a moral base of love, in which human beings and nature are valued not just for what advantage we can make of them, but more fundamentally for what they are. With his poetic sensibility, Borge seeks to lead beyond divisive stances ("humankind vs. nature") by fostering an awareness that love of nature and love of humankind are mutually reinforcing attitudes.

This symposium on saving Lake Xolotlán, which we propose to name Lake of the Nations, would not have been possible under *somocismo.*[1] Generally speaking, it would also not have been possible under capitalism. For although similar symposia are held under capitalism, and although capitalist governments take measures to limit the plundering of nature, the basic reality is that those who possess the means of transforming nature—the owners of machines, factories, agricultural estates—the capitalists, that is—are the primary despoilers of nature. For that reason, the historic initiative for saving nature has arisen from the people, and in opposition to governments that represent capitalists.

Antipollution measures adopted by capitalist governments have a lot in common with laws intended to improve the lot of workers. These measures have always been either forcibly obtained through broad popular movements, or adopted because they resulted in economic benefit for the capitalist class as a whole, or because they served to stabilize the system. In general, though, the response of these governments to the destruction of nature does little more than reproduce the damage elsewhere: the very logic of the capitalist system entails such destruction.

VALUING HUMAN BEINGS AND NATURE

If capitalism will not value human beings for themselves, how could it take interest in nature for its own sake? Capitalism views human beings only as a labor force, and nature as raw material for producing merchandise. Capitalism conceives of the world as an immense marketplace, whose activity has but one purpose: to accumulate profits in the pockets of capitalists. What does it matter to a lumber company that it is transforming a forest into a desert, if the sale of the lumber is profitable? What does it matter to a chemical manufacturing company that it is poisoning a river, if its products are selling well? What difference does it make to a mining company if it is poisoning rivers with cyanide?

Our view of nature is entirely different. Human beings do not abruptly end where their organic bodies end. For without nature, human beings are nothing, just as nature would be nothing without human beings. Humankind was made for nature, and above all nature was made for humankind; nature is the inorganic body of humankind, complementing the organic body. Human beings live from nature not only physically, but also spiritually. What is art but nature that human beings have made their own in forms expressing beauty? What is science but nature that human beings have made their own through thought? But for nature to be the inorganic body of humankind, humans have to transform it, humanize it. This is a process that extends over centuries, over all human history.

"Our fauna is symbolic of the freedom won
by the revolution."

What characterizes capitalism in this regard is that it uses the discoveries of humankind to dehumanize nature, even going so far as to render it inhuman. How can human beings feel they are part of nature when they must breathe the smog of big cities? How can human beings feel fulfilled by nature transformed into biochemical weaponry and neutron bombs? There are those who orient their philosophy, their science, their political will, and their practice to destroy nature and likewise to destroy human beings, and who become furious when human beings decide to save nature and to save other human beings.

REFLECTIONS IN THE LAKE

In our case the capitalist destruction of nature is epitomized in the present condition of Lake Managua. The importance of this lake stands out clearly: on the one hand, its strategic location in a region containing almost a quarter of the population of the country, and about 40 percent of the urban population; a region containing the country's greatest productive investments, along with its best and most extensive infrastructure.

On the other hand, nature could not have been more generous with us, having made a gift of such tremendous potential benefits in our two great lakes. Lake Managua in particular offers possibilities as to drinkable water, fisheries, irrigation for the country's best soil, energy where it is in greatest demand, and finally recreation, tourism, and beauty. And what did *somocismo* do with this lake? Or in other words, what did imperialism and its local agents do during the forty-odd years that the Somoza dictatorship functioned as its instrument of domination in Nicaragua?

Obviously, some problems have natural causes, as in the case of salification compounded by the lack of significant drainage. The creation of an outlet that would allow us to take advantage of the energy and irrigation potentials of Lake Xolotlán is the most arduous task posed by nature itself. Of course, this was of no concern to *somocismo,* because imperialism and its servants were interested only in fast and easy gain, and for the local, dependent capitalism these gains became a matter of urgency in the rush of local overseers to grab for themselves the crumbs and extras left them by the sated masters [of First World capitalism]. What interest, then, could *somocismo* have in a long-term project in which the common benefit outweighed the private benefit?

That, then, is the natural problem. But this problem has been artificially compounded by capitalist activity in the lake's watershed. As engineers, agronomists, geologists, specialists in the many branches of science and production, you have already examined the various components of the problem in detail. I shall therefore limit myself to setting forth the most general aspects of the problem, emphasizing the revolutionary perspective on the question before us.

First, we need to stress the effects on the surrounding watershed of the type of agriculture imposed on us by the imperialist requirements of the global market. The intensified cultivation of coffee, sugar, and above all, cotton, entailed the progressive loss of the natural vegetational cover, especially from the 1950s onward. It should be remembered that coffee, sugar, and cotton are crops foreign to our soil, so that the capitalist intensification of these crops set in motion a process of destruction of our ecosystem, further hampering our development. The result was leaching of sediments into the lake. Moreover, technological dependency led the country to import such products as long-lived pesticides, which ran off into the lake with the sediments.

Then, with the effort in the 1960s to establish a program of import-substitution, there appeared all those factories that, in keeping with the logic of capitalism, began to fill the lake with untreated, toxic industrial wastes. And to complement this capitalist productive anarchy, this selfish anarchy that disregards any common interest, we find a government that joyfully resolves the problem of sewage by dumping it into the lake, where decomposition of the enormous volume of organic matter depletes dissolved oxygen in addition to causing bacteriological contamination—a government that, in the last analysis, demonstrates its "concern" for the public welfare by transforming the lakeshore into a hideous garbage dump.

The result has been to transform the long-term, natural problem of saving the lake into an immediate, urgent matter.

THE ECOLOGY OF SELFISHNESS

Little did it matter to the capitalists, who amassed their wealth with the sweat of the collectivity in their factories and cotton plantations, what was to befall a collective good. Little did it matter to them what happened to the 250 fisher families who live off the contaminated fish of Xolotlán. To the capitalists, who could use their profits from ecocide to enjoy the beaches of Miami, little did it matter that they were depriving the poor of Managua of the beauty and recreation provided them by nature with the gift of Xolotlán. It is interesting to note in passing that as the rich fled to the Masaya Highway and south, the poor of Managua have held fast to the polluted lakeshores, as they would to debris from a shipwreck.

Not only did none of this matter to our second-class capitalists: they actually went so far as to actively oppose the possibility of forestalling the destruction of our lake. Some conscientious intellectuals advocated the substitution of biological controls for the pesticide contaminants. That led representatives of the pesticide manufacturers to join with the *somocista* Ministry of Agriculture in a holy crusade that, naturally, was to crown itself with the trophy of an ever more sickly ecosystem.

But imperialism did not have time here to complete the ecocide of which it can pride itself in other countries. In Europe, in its cradle, capitalism has had time to completely contaminate the Rhine, the Danube, those great rivers that poets, composers, and ancient chroniclers have taught us to admire. In the United States, where more than anywhere else "time is money," capitalism has taken but a few years to achieve the ecocidal work for which Europe required centuries. Now the transnational corporations have sought to extend the destruction elsewhere, as in the case of the Penwalt Corporation, whose chlorine and caustic soda factory dumped an estimated forty tons of toxic mercury into our lake. Add to this the sedimentation from eroded soils, the leaching of pesticides, the raw sewage from forty years of *somocismo,* the percolations from the garbage piled on the beaches, and you can see how Somoza sought to turn both the lake and all of Nicaragua into a sewer. Nicaragua is sick on account of that inheritance, just as is the lake. And though the illness didn't have time enough to progress to the terminal stage, the ecocidal work of imperialism and its local associates has seriously complicated the natural problem of salification and lack of drainage.

These are the outlines of the problem, the broad essentials that need to be taken into account in order to correctly formulate and resolve the problem.

REVOLUTIONARY ECOLOGY

Let's now have a look at the proposals, the practical steps toward a solution, that have been under discussion in this symposium.

Above all, it is obvious that the first step has been taken with the revolution itself. Our basic problem is that of underdevelopment, and with the attainment of political power we have gained the possibility of resolving it, a possibility completely denied us under the conditions of imperialist domination. In particular, our newly-won political power opens up the possibility of saving our lake.

Political power in Nicaragua no longer represents the private interests of a few transnational corporations and their local overseers: it now represents the interests of the majority of the population, the interests of the people. Proposals for saving the lake were also considered under *somocismo,* but only proposals that were agreeable to the bourgeois minority in power or their accomplices. These were one-sided proposals, which—in typically capitalist fashion—acknowledged nothing beyond questions of profitability, without taking into account consequences for the whole of our economy, the whole of our ecosystem, and above all, the consequences for the happiness and recreation of the people. This view is caricatured in an extreme example recalled by *compañero* Moisés Hassan, the case of an engineer (who I think was German) who proposed drying out the lake to convert the lakebed into land for cultivation.

Whichever proposal is finally adopted for the purpose of saving the lake, it must be based on all the interests at stake, on the common good. It should yield broad economic benefit instead of profit for a minority, and should concern itself with all potential benefits, including fisheries, energy, and irrigation; it should make allowance for the esthetic joy and recreation of our people, without falling into pure antieconomic estheticism; and finally, it must keep in mind the limited resources at our disposal, as well as possible means of foreign assistance.

The second step toward a solution of this problem is the one we have jointly undertaken—the government by organizing this symposium, and yourselves by bringing it to fruition. This step looks to the creation of a broader consciousness of the problem, to further discussion and investigation in order to bring us to the proposal that best synthesizes and coordinates the aforementioned requirements, and to the most suitable methods and instruments for carrying it out.

Some of the conclusions you have reached show that we have already started on the path leading to the objective sought by this symposium and by others to follow. First, it is clear that in the short run we must proceed with efforts to halt the process of contamination, that we must proceed with reforestation, that we must alter sewage disposal arrangements to prevent raw sewage from reaching the lake, that we must push forward with biological pest controls, that we must enact legislation to mandate treatment of industrial wastes (the engineer Rappacciolli has promised to head the effort once the Momotombo geothermal plant goes on line), and finally, that we must regulate the agricultural exploitation of the lake's watershed.

Secondly, in an intermediate stage, it is beyond doubt that the restoration of the lake will require the infusion of a large volume of water from outside. The most advanced proposal in this respect is one that would transfer water from Lake Cocibolca to Lake Xolotlán. However, there is also the possibility of bringing this mass of water from elsewhere, from the Matagalpa River, for example, as one of the speakers has suggested. In any case it is clear that we need to bring in water from somewhere. Moreover, whatever the system selected, it must allow for multiple use of the waters and must not destroy any ecosystem.

Thirdly, there is a pressing need to create an interagency committee that would bring together the interests of the various agencies—irrigation, energy, fishing, recreation, and so forth. This committee would be charged with coordinating all efforts relating to the lake, including research, planning, formulation of proposals, and execution and administration of projects. A committee with sufficient authority to take on the immediate task of stopping the contamination, to take charge of reducing the leaching of sediments, to stop the dumping of industrial wastes, to investigate appropriate technologies in support of our national industry and to reduce dependence on external sources, to take charge of guiding the steps of each particular agency (as for example getting INAA to move on the treatment of raw sewage), pressuring them to come up with concrete proposals to present to international organizations likely to provide aid.

POPULAR PARTICIPATION

None of these steps—as in the case of all the other steps our revolution is taking, as in the enormous step that our revolution itself signifies—can be securely achieved without popular participation. I think you are all in agreement on this. The Sandinista Popular Revolution is none other than our people in action. Without popular participation, all our efforts run the risk of losing the social content that ensures that such efforts will be truly revolutionary.

For this reason all plans and projects should be translated into the language of the people, explained to the people. The people should be able to understand that the problem you are discussing at a scientific and technical level is a basic problem affecting everyday life. The people should be able to understand that what's at stake is the satisfaction of its interests, and that such satisfaction doesn't just drop out of the sky, but has to arise out of a venture in which the people participates as principal protagonist. Without the people as principal protagonist, our revolution would not have been possible. Similarly, without the participation of the people, it won't be possible to save the people's lake.

This means that in addition to listening to the explanations of the experts, the people must in turn contribute its own experience; we must make the proposals come alive by involving the people in the discussions. We should, for example, submit proposals for critical review by the 250 fisher families who make up the hamlet of San Francisco del Carnicero and other communities. Above all, we must submit these proposals to discussion by the residents of Managua.

It is obvious that the CDSs [Sandinista Defense Committees, neighborhood-based participatory organizations involved in crime-detection, revolutionary vigilance, vaccination and sanitation campaigns, etc.] and other popular organizations must perform a decisive role here in bringing these matters to the attention of the people, and in transmitting anxieties felt at the grassroots to higher levels. It would even be appropriate to think of other mechanisms such as referenda to stimulate and facilitate popular participation, without which it is impossible to fulfill the revolutionary program.

PURSUING THE VISION OF SANDINO AND ST. FRANCIS

Compañeros, our revolution was born in the mountains; they were our first ally in the fight against *somocismo*. The nature that imperialism destroyed in the city is the same nature that gained its revenge by hiding us revolutionaries in the mountains, effacing our footprints, resisting efforts to clear away forest cover through cutting and burning, and rendering itself impenetrable to the bombardments of the enemy. In the mountains, we the children of Sandino entered into a pact with nature, and now we must fulfill our part.

The dictatorship that imperialism imposed on us could not break the ties that exist between us and nature. It didn't have time to form those great metropolises where nature is barely recognizable in some sickly trees, or in trees growing in parks like animals in a zoo. It was in the mountains that we came to understand that the imperialism that destroys human lives finds its complement in the imperialism that destroys nature.

The imperialists will once again wonder how we could be holding symposia such as these in a period of national emergency.[2] They likewise wondered how, amid the battles in the mountains and the tortures in the jails, we could have had the time to write poems and songs to our fallen *compañeros,* to our mothers, to our children, to our lovers. They cannot understand any of this, for none of this can find a place in mercantile logic.

For us it's enough that we understand each other, that we know where we come from. We come from the dreams of all those who loved humanity because they loved nature, and loved nature because they loved humanity. We come from the dreams of Sandino, of Carlos Fonseca, and we know where we are going, we are going toward that society in which we could—like Saint Francis—say to the sun, "brother sun," to the moon, "sister moon," to the star, "sister star," and to human beings, "brother and sister human beings."

We are moving toward a society in which Lake Xolotlán will no longer be a mere silver legend praised in song, but a transparent reality in which the blue of the sky is reflected together with the green of the most lovely flower and fruit garden in Central America; and over its shores, filled with the laughter of our children, Momotombo, "father of fire and stone," will raise his watchful head.[3]

The *somocismo* that murdered tens of thousands of Nicaraguans also tried to murder Lake Xolotlán, but just as Somoza couldn't kill the people, he couldn't kill the lake. We Nicaraguan revolutionaries would be irresponsible and stupid if we were to let our lake die. What's more I think we would cease to be revolutionaries if we weren't to save the lake and transform it into a source of production, of irrigation, of energy, and of beauty.

The most important achievement of this symposium is to have raised consciousness about the need to save our lake. Saving the lake is for Nicaragua a question of "a free homeland or death."

NOTES

1. The lake on whose southern flank Managua is situated is called Lake Managua or Lake Xolotlán. It empties by way of a short river into the largest lake in Central America, Lake Nicaragua or Lake Cocibolca.

2. The national emergency was a result of a marked increase in U.S. military assistance to the armed counterrevolution, which began spreading death and destruction throughout the more remote parts of the country.

3. Momotombo is a volcano overlooking the lake and city of Managua. With Italian assistance, the revolutionary government has built the country's first geothermal power plant on its slopes. Momotombo I went on line in 1983 with 35 MW, and Momotombo II, which will provide another 35 MW, is under construction.

10

The Revolution Confronts
the Theology of Death
(1982)

*On May 31, 1982, Tomás Borge addressed the Third Congress of
the World Conference of Christians for Peace in Central America
and the Caribbean, held in Managua. It was a time of rapidly
escalating tension as the Reagan administration began large-scale
military assistance to* contra *armed forces organized under the
leadership of former National Guard officers. The tension was
further fueled by Miguel Obando y Bravo, archbishop of Managua, when, in a Holy Week homily that immediately preceded
Borge's speech, he declared that Jesus had called Judas a* compañero, *the form of address used among Sandinistas.*

*Obando's scriptural reference was to Matthew 26:50, where
Jesus responds to Judas's betrayal with "Friend, why are you
here?" (RSV). The statement is altogether absent from the Gospels
of Mark and John, and is rendered as "Judas, would you betray the
Son of Man with a kiss?" (RSV) in Luke's Gospel (22:48). Even in
Matthew, however, Jesus' form of address is never authoritatively
translated as* compañero, *"companion": the* Revised Standard
Version *and* New English Bible *concur in the usage of* friend, *as
does the* Nueva Biblia Española *in its selection of* amigo.

What is more, the root meaning of compañero *is that of sharing
bread (*pan *in Spanish), an act of the most profound Christian
significance. It is therefore all the more interesting that the San-*

dinistas have chosen this form of address over that used by conventional communist parties: camarada, *or* comrade, *whose root meaning has to do with sharing the same bedroom or barracks.*

What is so important about this address is that a revolutionary comandante *reveals a far deeper understanding of the gospel than his adversary the archbishop, who has since been elevated to the rank of cardinal. In the pages that follow, Tomás Borge goes far beyond narrow (and misrepresented) citations to resurrect some major prophetic themes. Centering his perspective in Jesus' pivotal parable of the great judgment, he distinguishes between the theology of life ("as you have fed, clothed, sheltered these, the least of my brethren, so have you done to me") and its opposite, the theology of death. Using Jesus' own criteria for discernment, he offers a penetrating analysis of Nicaraguan—and by inference, Latin American—church and society.*

THE SOCIAL STRUCTURES OF HELL

It is no secret to you that in Nicaragua as elsewhere in Latin America natural disasters are not the principal human tragedy. Such calamities—hurricanes, earthquakes, droughts—are not our peoples' principal source of suffering. It hasn't even been war itself, but rather our social structures, that, instead of forming the basis for an earthly paradise, have generated an artificial hell on earth to which millions of human beings are subjected. In Asia, Africa, and Latin America, and even in the developed capitalist countries themselves, there is hunger and thirst for justice. Banishing hunger, injustice, exploitation, and the denial of life is the same thing as securing peace; it is the fundamental duty of humankind. All peoples share in this obligation to combat the existence of hell and find the keys to an earthly paradise.

The Nicaraguan people has made its contribution to this tremendous historical struggle. On its own soil it has defeated the historical enemy of humankind—imperialism and its faithful deputies, the *vendepatrias* [those who would "sell their homeland"].

DREAMS OF GUERRILLA FIGHTERS

Achieving victory was, as you know, difficult; consolidating the victory is, as you likewise know, extremely difficult. It is by now common knowledge that we encountered a country eviscerated by decapitalization, mortgaged by an enormous foreign debt, with an obsolete productive base. Our first efforts were directed to the recovery of production to establish a base for structural transformation. We initially erred on the side of voluntarism, because—amid the dreams and ideals we harbored in the tempestuous course of the guerrilla war and the clandestine struggle—we thought it would be possible to eliminate our backwardness and poverty rapidly. Without ever renouncing the dreams that made our revolution possible, we have come to understand that objective conditions—economic dependency, the nature of productive structures, our extraordinary technical, scientific, and cultural limitations—cannot be eliminated by decree, and that they comprise a heavy weight that burdens the speed and rhythm of transformation.

POPULAR STRUGGLE AND RELIGION

We had of course foreseen the existence of the counterrevolution as an inevitable response to the revolution, and we certainly foresaw the role U. S. imperialism would assume in it in the face of the transformation set in motion by the Sandinista Popular Revolution. Without any doubt the counterrevolution, armed with guns and an ideology of deceit and alienation, and with the open participation of imperialism, likewise constitutes an objective restraint on our development, because a large part of our efforts, resources, and cadres have been directed to the defense of the revolution.

The struggle between the interests of the people and the interests of the rich extends into every realm including the religious. It is no secret that the majority of Nicaraguans are Christian; it is likewise no secret that a majority of Nicaraguans are Sandinistas, just as it is no secret that the leaders and representatives of this Christian and revolutionary people are profoundly respectful of religious beliefs, of freedom of conscience. Neither is it a secret what role the upper ecclesiastical hierarchy has assumed in the face of our revolution and in the face of our people.

CHURCH AND STATE IN *SOMOCISMO*

In this context, it is good to consider what is and what should be the relationship between the church and the revolutionary state.

Obviously, the nature of this relationship must be shaped by the nature of the new state. The *somocista* state functioned as an instrument of repression against the interests of the people as a whole, and the relationship that existed between church and state was dominated by this concrete reality. Somoza encouraged the ecclesiastical hierarchy to defend the interests of the exploiting classes; he showed no scruples in instrumentalizing the most sacred religious sentiments in order to institutionalize the submission of workers. At times *somocismo* achieved its aims, to the point where the founder of the dynasty was named "prince of the church," and on many occasions the most renowned criminals of the regime, including Somoza himself, ate at the same table and exchanged toasts with the hierarchs of the Catholic Church. In spite of this, numerous priests took no part in *somocismo* and faithfully remained alongside their people. There were some, however, who assumed military posts, or who did not hesitate in profaning their sacred ministry by becoming chaplains in an army that distinguished itself by its systematic violation of all the commandments and moral norms of Christianity.

It was only logical that the state as repressor of the interests of the Christian people should seek to convert religion into an instrument of spiritual repression and a potent opiate for the people. All this explains why our Christian people had no recourse but to go to the catacombs, why our Christian people—rebelling against those who were deforming religion—began to understand it as an instrument of liberation, as a commitment to justice, to liberty, and to a change in the prevailing structures. That is why Christians went into hiding, as well as why they shouldered the rifle of liberty; that is why the Christian people, without ceasing to be Christian, became Sandinista.

CHURCH AND STATE IN THE REVOLUTION

If the relationship between church and state during *somocismo* was conditioned upon the interests of exploiters and their repression, it is only natural and historically logical that the relationship between the revolutionary state and the church should be based on defending the interests of those who were exploited and oppressed, because the revolution and the revolutionary state defend those interests. We didn't carry out a revolution in order to maintain the repression of the people; the revolution was carried out to liberate the people, so that everyone would have the liberty to believe or not to believe, according to the dictates of individual consciences. The FSLN, in a public declaration regarding religion, said the following:

> The Revolutionary State, like every modern state, is a secular state and cannot establish any religion, because it is the representative of all the people, of believers and unbelievers alike.

This is why the revolution guarantees religious freedom, which means that those who offend against religious freedom are adopting a counterrevolutionary position, just as those who offend against freedom of conscience in general are adopting a counterrevolutionary position.

A banner hangs from scaffolding of the catheral in Estelí as it undergoes reconstruction from damage inflicted by the National Guard: "He removed the powerful from their thrones and placed the poor in their stead (Lk 1:52)."

FREEDOM TO WORSHIP GOD
BUT NOT THE GOLDEN CALF

But one must distinguish clearly between what constitutes religious freedom and what constitutes counterrevolutionary activity. In our country there is full freedom to worship God, but there is no freedom to worship the golden calf. In Nicaragua there is freedom to pray, to attend Mass, and to comply with the magnificent moral commandments of Christianity. But there cannot be freedom to conspire; there cannot be freedom to maintain relationships with (and accept firstfruits from) the U. S. Central Intelligence Agency; there cannot be freedom to deceive, to destabilize the country; there cannot be freedom to instrumentalize the religious sentiments of our people against the interests of the people; there cannot be freedom to utilize fraud, fetishism, and even the supernatural with the aim of reinstating the exploiting classes, together with imperialist domination of Nicaragua. How could we be so irresponsible, unpatriotic, and clumsy as to permit the liberty of telling our people it's a sin to defend the homeland and render homage to the flag and national anthem? We would completely lose our sense of history if we did not confront the savagery and the trumped-up visions that, abusing the name of Christ and the Virgin Mary, strive to draw water to the mill of the counterrevolution.

ANTI-CHRISTIAN APOSTLES

In these days of great suffering for our people—though of even greater confidence and optimism—we have seen the perverse and criminal influence some religious sects are exercising over the inhabitants in numerous locales around the country. I myself witnessed some infirm poor persons who wouldn't leave their homes when menaced by floodwaters, owing to the advice of religious leaders who were telling them that all this had been the fruit of God's will, that God would protect them, and that they would not need the help of the Sandinistas. We have known cases in which some persons refused medical attention because they thought it would be a sin and because the Sandinistas are "instruments of the devil." In a number of churches some have even insinuated that natural disasters are God's punishment for the course taken by our revolutionary process.

To be sure, those who promote such works aren't true Christians; I think they are better described as anti-Christians. And if these currents should come to have a common leader, in all justice we would have to give him the title Antichrist.

The false apostles and the Antichrist are bearers of a philosophy alien to true Christianity. These are the ones who preach traditional charity—"bandaid" charity—debasing the true nature of Christian charity. Charity means love, but the charity that has been preached here is the charity of alms and bread crusts. It's the charity of *nacatamales* on anniversaries and weekends; it's the charity of feeding the hungry and perpetuating their hunger; it's the charity of the elegant lady who extends her freshly manicured hand to deposit a coin in the portal of the church; it's the charity of the powerful who make last-minute calls to create local support groups and to collect some blankets and clothes cast aside by their members because they are already out of style, and to get rid of some canned goods that are worth far less than what they pay to have their columns published in the newspaper.[1]

OUR PEOPLE: THE SAMARITAN

It wasn't the Levite but the Samaritan who aided the traveler plundered and wounded by thieves. The Samaritan is today the symbol of our people. The Samaritan represents the highest expression of *compañerismo*. The first Christians understood by *neighbor* what we express as *compañero*. This led them, in the true sense of Christian charity, not to contribute what they didn't need, but rather to share their goods. I believe Nicaraguan Christians have only now retrieved the original meaning of charity, the true meaning of *compañerismo*.

This brings to mind the distortion that a leading hierarch of the church recently made of the word *compañero*.[2] He said that Christ had called his disciples brothers and had uniquely addressed Judas, the traitor, as *compañero*. I think the person who said this either doesn't know or pretends not to know the true significance of *compañero*. *Compañero* is the one who shares; *compañeros* are those who give of themselves, who are capable of sharing their love, their charity, even to the point of giving their very lives. Thousands upon thousands of Christians died in Nicaragua with the word *compañero* on their lips; those who shared bread and work called each other *compañero. Compañera* is the mother of her children; *compañeros* are brothers—although at times there are brothers who are not *compañeros:* Carlos Fonseca [Amador] and Fausto Amador weren't *compañeros,* and Cain and Abel weren't *compañeros,* and Judas Iscariot could never have been a *compañero* of Christ. I think the person who said that is a militant counterrevolutionary, someone who aspires to be Antichrist.

CONFRONTING THE THEOLOGY OF DEATH

The protagonists of the old charity, the charity with which they sought to deform our conscience, are the champions of the theology of death. All who side with the exploiters, whether in the name of religion or any other principle, are accomplices in the misery and hunger of our people—the misery and hunger that have prepared a premature death for millions of human beings; the misery and hunger that have provoked the rebellion of the oppressed, and the genocide and violence of oppressors; the misery and hunger that is the philosophy of imperialism to subdue the peoples of the Third World.

To confront the theology of death, authentic Christians have proposed the theology of resurrection—but, from what I've understood, not the resurrection of the dead but the resurrection of the living. Authentic Christians believe that emerging from the tomb cannot be reduced to merely returning to life, but entails being reborn, *transformed.* And this is why the point of contact—better yet, the integration of liberationist Christianity with revolution—is happening in our national revolution, because the political agenda of this liberation is none other than the agenda of life. . . . Life is the only force capable of transforming the world, and I am speaking of life in historical terms. A miserable existence is not life. Exploitation and its complement of misery are more like death than like life.

THE GOD OF LIFE

I believe you Christians have very well grasped the significance of the fact that Yahweh is God of the living, not God of the dead. To be alive is to be in a state of vigor, happiness, and health, in a vibrant culture. That is why what Saint Paul says in one of his epistles is so true: that property held in common is life, and the opposite is slavery and death.[3] And Christianity affirms Yahweh as eternally alive, confronting the gods of death. To John the Apostle, life is the fullest expression of freedom, and that is why true Christianity, the true historical agenda of Jesus Christ, is resurrection and life. Every exploitive undertaking, every plan conceived against the people, regardless of the clothing in which it is dressed, intrinsically bears the logic of death. In the archetype of the opposite theology and in every endeavor that encompasses human liberation is borne the logic of life. Here we proclaim the right to life. The human being is meant to be born into life, not into death; that is why those who sacrificed their blood, who were capable of being helpful to their last breath, continue to live.

The reign of Jesus Christ is rightly considered the reign of life; the reign of Satan—that is to say, the reign of oppression and slavery—is the reign of death.[4]

" I WAS HUNGRY, AND YOU FED ME"

When Christ, according to Saint Matthew, said [Matt. 25:31–46]: "I was hungry and you fed me, I was thirsty and you gave me drink, I was a stranger and you took me in, I was naked and you clothed me, I was imprisoned and you came to visit me," that did not mean we should pass around some sandwiches on our birthdays. It holds a much deeper meaning. How can one feed the hungry without freeing them from tyranny and foreign oppression? How can one feed the hungry and clothe the naked without developing the means of production for the benefit of the people? Feeding the hungry and clothing the naked can be achieved only by way of profound economic transformations. The best implementation of this Christian principle is to set in motion a profound and revolutionary agrarian reform. How are we to clothe the naked without developing textile production? How are we to visit prisoners without constructing a profoundly humane penitentiary system? How are we to welcome the stranger without developing a spirit of revolutionary solidarity in the minds and hearts of human beings? This is what distinguishes us from the pharisees, from those who seek to reach heaven tranquilizing their consciences with miserable handouts. This is what the revolution is going to do to feed the hungry, who hunger not only for bread but above all for justice and liberation.

WHY ARE THEY FEARFUL?

This answer our revolution has given is precisely what is terrorizing imperialism and the dominant classes in Latin America. It is what terrorizes their ideologues and decorated representatives. The power of example of the Nicaraguan revolution is not only in the way we chose to seize power. It was not only the armed struggle that was the "bad example" we gave the people, but also the position of the Sandinista Front on religion. It must be terribly distressing to them that in its formal declaration on the matter, the National Directorate of the FSLN affirms:

> The liberty to manifest religious faith is an inalienable right of all persons, which the Revolutionary Government fully guarantees. This principle has been on record for a long time in our revolutionary program and will be sustained in the future. . . . Our experience demonstrates that when Christians, drawing on their faith, are capable of responding to the needs of their people and of history, their very beliefs impel them to revolutionary militancy. Our experience shows us that one can be at the same time a believer and an effective revolutionary.

The Sandinista Front must have shattered a number of schemes and complicated the search for pretexts to oppose it when it asserts that "Christian *militantes* have every right to publicly express their convictions without its impairing their participation in the *Frente Sandinista de Liberación Nacional* or the confidence they have won through their revolutionary work." All of you know that there are a great number of Christians in the ranks of the *Frente Sandinista,* and that it is no coincidence that several Catholic priests—all devoted Christians—are members of the Sandinista Assembly.[5]

The Nicaraguan revolution has demonstrated that Christians and non-Christians can work together for a common objective, and has demonstrated there can be an integration between Christian moral principles and revolutionary moral principles. That is why the theologians of death are fighting, as open peons of U.S. imperialism, against the Nicaraguan revolution, so much does it signify by way of example to the Christians of Latin America. This explains why some sectors of the upper ecclesiastical hierarchy have assumed an attitude of persecution against progressive Christians and against the Sandinista Popular Revolution.

WHO PERSECUTES AND KILLS PRIESTS?

In other Latin American countries, priests who are identified with the people are murdered, tortured, kidnapped, and exiled. Archbishop Romero is not the only priest to have been murdered in Latin America, though his death was a particularly resplendent sign of light and blood. In all of Latin America, including Nicaragua, progressive priests are driven out. But who in our country has expelled these progressive priests and nuns? Not the revolutionary government, but the theologians of death. Who are the ones who persecute progressive priests in Nicaragua? Not the Sandinista police, so slandered in the elegant temples of the bourgeoisie; it's been the theologians of death, it's been Torquemada.[6] Certain religious structures look more and more like tribunals of the Inquisition, in spite of the fact that in these high-ranking bodies—let's be fair about it—there are some judicious, patriotic, and Christian members. These, along with innumerable Catholic priests and Evangelical pastors, have become a part of the revolution because they have integrated themselves with the poor. They have taken part in a revolution that preaches virtue and condemns corruption and vice; they have joined a revolution that has liberated the country from foreign domination. They have become part of the most generous revolution in history, integrating themselves into this glorious moment our country is living. For them our profound respect and affection, our gratitude and admiration. . . .

FIGHTING FOR JUSTICE: FIGHTING FOR PEACE

We can, Christian *compañeros,* responsibly assure you that we are enemies of war; that we are advocates of negotiated solutions; that we will never launch an aggression against another country regardless of the differences we may have with its leaders; that we repudiate all forms of aggression, and that it is precisely for that reason that our revolution and our government has shown solidarity with Argentina, victim of imperial aggression for its attempt to reestablish sovereignty over all its territory. The path of justice is, in the last analysis, the path of peace, and once all the governments of the world become partisans of justice, builders of social justice, they will become builders of peace as well. To fight for peace we need to fight for justice. To fight for peace we need to combat the injustice encompassed by the aggression, the threats, the arrogance of the powerful. To fight for peace we need to fight so that the Christ of the poor is not crucified anew. To fight for peace we need to fight against conceit, against wrongdoing, against selfishness, against vice, against hatred, against treason, against vanity, against the repugnant instrumentalization of the crucifixion.

To fight for peace, Christian *compañeros,* we must be prepared to commit our very lives, we must be prepared to say, in full awareness of what is being said: "A free homeland or death!"

NOTES

1. *Nacatamales* are traditional Nicaraguan food consisting of maize and pork, wrapped in banana leaves. The paid column of the High Council of Private Enterprise (COSEP) is entitled "Ideas para todos" ("ideas for all"), and appears regularly in the pages of *La Prensa*. It features the ideas of free-market economists from Adam Smith to Milton Friedman. Number 86 in the series, entitled "Declarations of Principles of the Private Sector" (September 28, 1985), opened with a declaration that "economic freedom is an end in itself."

2. The hierarch was Archbishop—now Cardinal—Miguel Obando y Bravo. Further commentary is provided in the introduction to this selection.

3. Borge has evidently mistaken St. Paul for St. Peter (see Acts 2:44–47, 4:32–5:12).

4. More recently (*Barricada,* Oct. 27, 1984) Borge described the CIA terrorism manual distributed among the *contras* as "the Bible of Death."

5. The Sandinista Assembly is the top consultative body of the FSLN, not to be confused with the National Assembly, which is the Nicaraguan legislature.

6. Tomás de Torquemada (1420?–1498) was the infamous inquisitor-general in the Spanish Inquisition.

11

The Christian Foolishness of St. Francis
(1982)

On October 3, 1982, Tomás Borge took part in a peace march through Managua in commemoration of the 800th anniversary of the birth of St. Francis of Assisi. The march culminated inside the church of Santa María de los Angeles, in the lower-class neighborhood of Barrio Riguero. There, with Franciscan parish priest Uriel Molina Oliú by his side, Borge delivered the following address.

Here again, as in his earlier speech on law and social justice, Borge places Marxist analysis at the service of explicitly Christian values. Marxism is accepted not as a metaphysical system of final values but as a genuinely scientific methodology for the analysis of historical patterns and tendencies, by which to facilitate incarnation of Christian/Franciscan values by discriminate Christians and other persons of good will. Speaking in this instance to an audience better versed in Christian than in Marxist thought, Borge begins with an exposition of the economic and social relationships that conditioned the medieval world confronted by St. Francis.

Dear brothers and sisters:

As we were walking over here in the march for peace, someone asked me my view of its meaning. I see this march for peace primarily as an act of recovery of the most beautiful Christian symbols. Latter-day pharisees and profaners of the temple have sought to steal the symbols of Christianity; yet the people, with its sense of history and future, is recovering these symbols. Among the most magnificent of these is St. Francis of Assisi, who cannot

rightfully be appropriated by the rich, because he belongs entirely
to the poor.

It has been eight hundred years since the birth of St. Francis.
That is a long time—almost a millennium. The fact that after all
these years he is still remembered with singular respect, affection,
and admiration underscores his extraordinary character.

Borge speaking from podium in church of San Francisco
de los Angeles, Barrio Riguero, Managua

*"Francis of Assisi, saint, poet, and revolutionary, is committed
to the poor of today as well as yesterday."*

THE FEUDAL SETTING

To understand the kindly St. Francis—his exemplary life, his
attitude toward humankind—one must visualize him in the context
of the society into which he was born, with its feudal economic

relationships and corresponding social movements. St. Francis lived from 1182 to 1226, a time when the first signs of decomposition of the feudal system were making their appearance. A class of skilled artisans had sprung up to satisfy the demands of feudal masters, aristocrats, kings—the rich of that period. The power of these lords was intimately linked to their control of the land, through which they unmercifully exploited the serfs, the *campesinos* of the time. The feudal masters were landlords who compelled the landless serfs to work for them without wages, allowing them no more than a minimal share of the produce or a small parcel of land that they could tend only a day or two a week.

It was around the castles of princes, dukes, archdukes, and other aristocrats, and in the cities of Italy, that the accumulation of capital was just getting underway, an accumulation that would later provide a base for the emergence of capitalism and the bourgeoisie. The agents of that accumulation were the artisans whose skilled hands produced the clothing, weaponry, tableware, furniture, and other consumption needs of the aristocracy. These artisans were emerging as an independent sector of society, later to develop into the bourgeoisie. From the port of Venice, they traded throughout the Mediterranean basin.

In the service of their feudal masters, merchants sold young persons, especially women, into the harems of Syrian and Egyptian monarchs. These very traders, principally from Pisa, Genoa, and Venice, were those who derived the greatest economic benefit from the Crusades, wars fought in the name of recovering the Holy Lands, but whose essence was in no way religious. As on many other occasions in human history, religion was used as a cover for the dealings of unscrupulous merchants who enriched themselves by the blood and destruction of warfare.

In our time, the use of war to promote business has led to the fabulous profits made by international weapons manufacturers and brokers, with their vested interest in fomenting war in order to sell the wares of destruction and death. The Vietnam war, to cite but one example, represented an enormous stream of wealth— dollars stained with blood—for U.S. transnational corporations. We sometimes wonder whether these same corporations are involved in the efforts to foment warfare in Central America, in order to enrich themselves at the cost of the blood of Central Americans.

But to return to the time of St. Francis, the scant development of the sciences made the effects of epidemics and other natural disasters all the more devastating. Aristocrats and merchants took advantage of critical situations to hoard basic foods, then extract enormous profits from the ensuing speculation, all without the slightest concern for the hunger of the people.

The development of commerce and of the production of luxuries by artisans occurred in tandem with the growth in consumption by wealthy aristocrats, whose expanded appetites had to be accommodated by accentuating the exploitation of the serfs and the other lower strata of society, including artisans themselves. This meant the imposition of new taxes, and corresponding increases in repression against the people, against the poor. As the internal contradictions of society intensified, the feudal system began to come apart. (It is here we see the appearance of the famous knights errant, members of the nobility who undertook "amazing" feats—as they themselves saw it—such as carrying out armed assaults on the carriages of rich merchants, which were then publicized as heroic acts in the novels of the time.) The increase in exploitation led to armed uprisings by the lowest classes, which received substantial support from the artisans, and in some instances even from the merchants, because the depredations of the young nobles drove the merchants to seek shelter in the towns, or "burghs," as they were then called.

SEEDS OF CAPITALISM

With this influx the towns grew considerably in both population and importance. Significantly, it is from the word "burgh" that the term "bourgeoisie" later arose with the development of capitalism. In these towns a revolution was being born that would increasingly threaten the feudal system as production by artisans was converted into industrial production, as guildmasters were, little by little, transformed into capitalists, and as the overwhelming majority of artisans were transformed into wage-earners—that is to say, proletarians. Of course, industrial development was only in its most rudimentary phase at the time of St. Francis, evident only in the capitalist merchant who would place an order with a guildmaster, who would then hire salaried workers to fill the order. In time this would lead to the transformation of guildmaster into capitalist, but at the time of St. Francis guildmasters were still working artisans themselves.

With the development of productive forces and the initiation of struggle against the feudal system, the bourgeoisie began to gain strength as a social class (I realize this background material is rather dry, but it is necessary in order to understand what is coming), raising as its banner a demand for the elimination of feudal privileges and taxes. Later in its development, the bourgeoisie would trumpet the slogans of liberty, equality, and fraternity. Of course it had a particular concept of liberty in mind: the liberty of laissez-faire for developing the capitalist system of production, combined with the liberty to exploit salaried workers.

It can nonetheless be said that in that day the struggle of the bourgeoisie was of a progressive nature, because it was supplanting the even more backward system of feudalism. Of course, beginning with the overthrow of the feudal lords by the bourgeois revolutions several centuries later, there would arise a new struggle between the great capitalists and the workers. A new contradiction would then appear in the heart of society, a contradiction later resolved, as in Nicaragua today, by popular revolutions led by the working class.

But at the time of St. Francis it was the peasant movements that summoned the hungry masses to unyielding struggle, filled with bloodshed and great suffering, against the kings and nobles. Many of the leading hierarchs of the church were themselves princes, dukes, marquises, counts. All these species of aristocratic fauna were great landholders who enslaved the peasantry. So there were great contradictions within the church—as is the case today, and as always—and there were "disciples of Christ" who sided with the feudal lords, thereby proving themselves unauthentic disciples of Christ.

CHRISTIAN FOOLISHNESS

It is no accident that St. Francis founded a religious order around the "minors" or "small ones"—that is, the poor—as distinguished from the "great ones," the rich. With his extraordinary sensibility, Francis of Assisi, having been born into a line of wealthy merchants, knew the meaning of wealth, with its corollaries of selfishness and cruelty. His original name was John, but he adopted the name Francis as a pseudonym in his struggle on behalf of the poor. In his youth he had fought the German [Holy Roman] Empire, which then dominated Italy, much as Yankee imperialism dominates Latin America today. He fought the foreign invader, as did Sandino and Benjamín Zeledón, whose 133rd anniversary is also being observed today.[1] It was in the course of this war that Francis began to think about the selfishness of human beings, the wickedness of the rich, and the harsh life of the poor. This reflection was accompanied by an intensification of the love he felt for human beings, a love that grew to encompass all living beings and nature itself. St. Francis loved nature, loved life, loved to see joy in human beings.

St. Francis sided resolutely with the common folk, and for that reason founded the order of the Friars Minor. Being neither deacon nor priest, he had to consent to be ordained a deacon so that he might preach, and when asked whether he would prefer to join the Augustinian or Benedictine order, he replied, "I do not wish to belong to any order; I have had a divine revelation that I am a new fool" [in reference to 1 Cor. 1:18–28, 4:10]. This is the same designation later used against others who likewise fought for the poor and humble of the earth. St. Francis went beyond *preaching* love to *practicing* love; beyond *preaching* humility to *practicing* humility; beyond *preaching* identification with the poor to *sharing* their poverty. St. Francis sold all his possessions, including those inherited from his father, and distributed the proceeds among the poor, thereby joining the ranks of the poorest of the poor. . . .

So extraordinary a man as St. Francis could hardly have done otherwise in those days when the only humane response to human misery was to reduce consumption, to partake fully of the bread crusts and tattered clothing of poverty. In our time the proper thing to do is place the fruits of abundance that are the products of human labor within the reach of the people as a whole. St. Francis denounced inequality yet shared it; denounced hunger yet shared it. As Uriel Molina, this wonderful disciple of St. Francis, puts it, St. Francis was more a man of deeds than of words and preachments.

St. Francis created a world of *compañeros,* of brothers and sisters; a world that has ceased to be utopian in Nicaragua, and has at the very least been transformed into a serious enterprise. In this sense the ideal of St. Francis is being realized in Nicaragua on his 800th anniversary, just as someday it will be realized throughout Latin America, and someday the whole world will be blessed with human beings who love each other as brother and sister, just as St. Francis loved his fellow human beings [applause].

A CHURCH RENEWED

It would have been much easier for St. Francis to partake of the world of the aristocrats and wealthy merchants. It would have been much easier to preach the gospel of poverty while savoring the delicacies of a well-provided hearth. But he renounced the easy life of his native social class, leaving with no more than his coarse and worn woolen cloak, his serene eyes and gentle voice to journey about the world sharing his word, his tenderness, and his love for the poor and the weak.

St. Francis loved the sun and the stars, birds and trees, just as he loved human beings. Even when nearly blind, he sang to the sun, thanking the Lord God for the astral lights he could barely see; thanking God for the transparent and translucent forms of the sky, for brother wind, brother air, and sister cloud.

St. Francis of Assisi was a Christian committed to the poor, not only the poor of his time but the poor of today. Francis of Assisi, saint, poet, and revolutionary, is committed to your welfare as well [applause].

Many things have changed in Nicaragua, and Uriel has reminded us that the Christianity of yesteryear cannot endure. Though its essential core will remain, its forms of expression have to change; because there has been a revolution, creating a historical opportunity for church and revolution to collaborate in securing the happiness of the people [applause]. How, then, can we conceive of a Christianity of avarice and selfishness? How can we conceive of a Christianity that kneels before the feet of the powerful? How can we conceive of a Christianity that wafts incense to the powerful and brutal empire that is attacking us, threatening us, and seeking to destroy us? [applause]. There can be no such "Christianity" in Nicaragua! The only appropriate Christianity is one that appears as did St. Francis, as a herald of peace; a Christianity attired like St. Francis in coarse woolen cloth, that takes to the dirt roads to encounter the poor, to provide food for the hungry and consolation for the truly humble and afflicted of our earth [applause].

We must struggle so that there will no longer be two churches: the church of the sweat of the poor and the church of the expensive perfumes the rich buy in Europe! [applause]. We need to find a church that unites all those human beings for whom Jesus Christ and St. Francis died; a renewed church devoted to the humble, not a church kneeling before the golden calf; a church of the poor, a Franciscan church [applause]. St. Francis fought Emperor Frederick Barbarossa, the Reagan of his time; and Christians now must fight the Frederick of our time, supreme representative of the empire that seeks to destroy our revolution.[1] All Nicaraguans should jointly acquire the virtues of humility, love for the poor, and commitment to rescue the humble from their present misery.

Our great poet Rubén Darío wrote a poem to St. Francis. The poem describes how St. Francis tamed the beast, the terrible wolf of Gubbio that would emerge from its lair to kill with the spite of Lucifer, devouring sheep and shepherd alike. Though the wolf was an enemy of humankind, it returned to its den when confronted by the grief of St. Francis. We could say that the wolf is still lurking about its lair, with its frothing mouth and fierce eyes, and that the fires of Moloch and Satan still course through its blood. The wolf is on the loose, brother Francis, ravaging the border areas, killing, burning, torturing.

We ask you, brother Francis, to bestow on us your energy and your love with which to confront the mad and deadly wolf whose fangs are clothed in dollar bills and whose claws kill our children. That which your word alone could not achieve will be accomplished by your legacy, brother Francis. It is through love for the poor, through identification with workers and *campesinos,* with the humble of our earth, that we will derive the strength to destroy the wolf, offspring of the devil; to eradicate imperialism; to overcome the enemies of our people [applause]. The wolf is on the loose, but we Nicaraguan revolutionaries are going to destroy it [applause]. A free homeland! [response: Or death!].

NOTE

1. Frederick I Barbarossa (Italian for red-beard), Holy Roman emperor from 1155 to 1190, invaded Italy no less than five times (1154, 1158, 1163, 1166, 1174). He died while on a crusade to "recover the Holy Lands for the cross."

12

Christianity and Sandinism
(1983)

*In the course of an extended tour of Western Europe in 1983,
Borge addressed a theological congress held in Madrid in the
month of September.*

*In this, his most extended presentation on the subject to date,
Borge recounts the history of the two churches in Nicaragua: the
one that defended the common people and the other that named
Anastasio Somoza García a "prince of the church." He then relates
the story of the first contacts between priests and Sandinistas,
describing how mutual suspicion evolved into mutual respect and
revolutionary collaboration.*

*Especially noteworthy is Borge's masterful application of pro-
phetic scripture—from Isaiah, Micah, and Habakkuk in the Old
Testament to Jesus and James in the New—to an understanding of
the current revolutionary situation in Nicaragua. With this as a
base, he describes why and how the great imperial and ecclesiastical
powers of the day are trying to discredit and destroy this very
original revolution.*

Many are no doubt asking themselves: What is a former guerrilla
fighter who is now minister of the interior of revolutionary Nicaragua doing in a theological conference? Some answers have already
been suggested, but let me add my own.

The Sandinista revolution has been justifiably regarded as the most generous in history. It is a revolution without a death penalty, without tear gas canisters, and *with* open prisons and habeas corpus. It is a revolution of the poor, a revolution for peace and life.

Many of the moral principles of Christianity are the moral principles of the revolution applied to the concrete reality of Nicaragua. What, then, is so odd about having a representative of this revolution speak here? Why should it be strange that we are here among you, if in Nicaragua a process of convergence and identification has arisen between Sandinista revolutionaries and Christian revolutionaries? What is so strange about our presence, if many Sandinista revolutionaries are Christians and many Christians are Sandinista revolutionaries?

I am of course neither a theologian nor a priest, as reported by a news agency. I am a revolutionary from a country that is proud to have a land mass that is disproportionately small in relation to the reach of its poetry, its generosity, its revolution. And inasmuch as human beings and peoples pride themselves on their national distinctions, we Nicaraguans feel an obligation to forever continue being poets, being generous, being revolutionaries.

REVOLUTIONARY PRIESTS

In Latin America one sees ever more guerrilla fighters and theologians, combatants and priests, walking together through the same hardships, feeding themselves from the same poor plate of the popular struggles, and sharing an abundance of hopes. At times, priest and guerrilla fighter have coalesced in a single revolutionary, rising out of this Latin American history that broadens with every passing day, like the crowns of our tropical trees.

I refer not only to Camilo Torres, the pioneer [Colombian guerrilla-priest], or to Ernesto Cardenal in the peasant community of Solentiname, or to the Christian community that emerged around the university students in Managua's Barrio Riguero, or to the assassinated Guatemalan priests, or to [guerrilla *comandante* and priest] Gaspar García Laviana, or to Bishop Oscar Romero. I am also referring to Fray Bartolomé de Las Casas [who boldly took up the cause of the native inhabitants of New World lands conquered by Spain]; to Bishop Antonio Valdivieso, who was crucified [for championing the rights of the native peoples] by the Contrera brothers, Nicaragua's first tyrants; and to Miguel Hidalgo and José María Morelos, "guerrilla-priests" [who led the struggle for Mexican independence], as they were called by Jacques Lafaye.

If the cross and the sword were weapons of colonial domination, the cross and the rifle have frequently revindicated the right and obligation of Christians to identify with the poor.

THE THEOLOGY OF DEATH
AND THE THEOLOGY OF LIFE

In Nicaragua there are Christians who understand charity, love, and justice as the negation of hunger, illiteracy, economic backwardness, and dependency; there are Christians who disavow the alms provided by poor boxes in church vestibules—the charity, love, and justice reserved for weekends. In Nicaragua, there are Christians who clothe the naked by developing the textile industry, who feed the hungry by increasing the production of basic foods and by equitably distributing the nation's limited nutritional resources.

Nicaraguan Christians valiantly confront the heirs of those who consecrated Anastasio Somoza García's daughter Lilian "queen of the army," fitting her with the gold crown of the Virgin of Candelaria, and of those who designated the aged and cruel dictator "prince of the church."[1]

Braving the threat of excommunication, Nicaraguan Christians confront those who make offerings at the altar without seeking reconciliation; those who say they love God while with visceral hatred they devour both human beings and human principles, violating the second commandment of the gospel, to love one's neighbor.[2]

You cannot serve both God and riches. This of course means nothing to some individuals: to them gold is god; profits are god; the machine that vomits screws is god; the neutron bomb is god; deceit, if it is audacious, is god; indifference, silence, scorn of entreaties for peace and for the dead is god.[3] God is the one who throws out leftovers so that Lazarus may share them with the dogs of Epulon [Luke 16:19–21]; god is the Alliance for Progress, McCarthyism, the divine right to point the firepower of aircraft carriers at our coasts bristling not with missiles, but with unexploited spiny lobsters and miserable hovels.

These are the new gods of the society of consumption; the same gods that speak to the world through the one-way medium of television, with extraordinary lies that are transformed into truths by reason of the credibility attached to such media; they are the modern gods that have been able, thanks to the power of technology, to coexist with the contradictions of the tower of Babel.

The philosophy of these gods is that of death. The ideological expressions of the theology of death aim to encourage hopes that social transformation is completely determined from the heavens. Everything—including evil, tyranny, imperialism—can be disguised as the work of god. These divine decisions are unappealable.

THE BACKGROUND OF THE REVOLT

Like many other peoples around the world, the Nicaraguan people has been a victim of these illusions coldly devised to consolidate exploitation, to mock innocence, to tell lies, and justify human anguish. But in Nicaragua lies could no longer deceive the people. There was no alternative to the suffering and to combatting the violence—that is to say, other than to use violence to destroy the lies that were the causes of the violence.

The essential material conditions for derailing the violence in Nicaragua developed in the 1950s, in the course of a sinister and inevitable restructuring of the international capitalist system encompassing all Latin America. The capitalist development of the countryside for the production of cotton brought about a process of expropriation that deprived peasants and artisans of their means of production. Gone was the day when they could tolerate exploitation with a mentality in which nonconformity was not even a concept.

Industrial development in urban areas initiated in the 1960s was unable to absorb the masses migrating from the countryside in search of employment, electricity, betterment, or who knows what. Instead, their expectations gave way to cardboard shacks on the outskirts of our cities.

During the 1950s the popular revolutionary movement evolved toward armed forms of struggle. Some of the armed movements were still led by sectors of the bourgeoisie that opposed Somoza and came to believe that armed revolt was easy, and that the provisions for confronting battle fatigue could be purchased in the supermarket. These were the last efforts of this class to sustain an effective opposition to the dictatorship. The Nicaraguan bourgeoisie was characterized by a lack of unity and ideological organization, an absence of strategic and tactical vision, and a tendency to stridency, to a crass extravagance. The revolutionary sectors meanwhile sought to learn from their own experiences. On July 23, 1961, under the guidance of Carlos Fonseca, the FSLN was founded.

Statue of Andrés Castro in front of the cathedral in Masaya.
When his rifle misfired in an 1856 battle against U.S. invaders
under William Walker, he killed one of the mercenaries with a rock.

FIRST CONTACTS BETWEEN PRIESTS AND SANDINISTAS

The first contacts between Sandinista revolutionaries and Catholic priests were marked by personal cordiality, coupled with political and ideological distrust. We were lacking in faith, but we immersed ourselves in the waters until common sense and the survival instinct helped us make the encounter work.

Initially we Sandinistas sought Christian aid to ensure that a revolutionary victory, which seemed distant yet inevitable, would not turn into a bloodbath; it was a matter of foresight to forestall vengeance. By this I mean to say that the first contacts were of a tactical nature. Christians feared we might try to instrumentalize their faith on behalf of a political objective. And looking back on that first fraternal yet hesitant embrace, I see that for my part I was afraid they might finally convince me of the existence of the hell that Bishop Isidro Oviedo had described to inflame my fears. It seems to me that neither Carlos Fonseca nor any of us ever imagined that the exchange of letters with Ernesto Cardenal, and the positive dialogues with Father Uriel Molina, would produce anything beyond a mutual understanding, a search for sanctuary or some clerical denunciation of Somoza.

Though we engaged in philosophical discussions, it was with mutual astonishment that we found ourselves discovering it was more important to discuss the geography of love—a shared love for those they called the people of God and we called workers and peasants.

We were certain of the truth of St. Hilary's assertion: "The wealthy are either thieves or sons of thieves."[4] It wasn't long before it dawned on us that the rich had to disappear not as human beings but as exploiters, precisely so that they might recover their humanity, or at the very least, so that the poor could become human beings.

CHRISTIANS AND SANDINISTAS WORKING TOGETHER

The FSLN's pivotal role in the revolution was instrumental in the evolution of new forms of understanding between Christians and the vanguard political organization. The *Frente Sandinista* assembled what we called intermediate organizations, a means of coordination with a variety of other organizations: labor unions, groups of artists, student associations, and women's groups. The formation of Christian communities that attracted youth to a faith that included identification with the poor, brought them closer to the *Frente Sandinista* with its unequivocal option for the exploited.

This drawing together of revolutionary classes from similar but different positions led us to designate Christian youth groups as intermediary organizations, as umbilical cords to the people.

This moment marked the beginning of a dialectical relationship between cadres of the *Frente Sandinista* helping with work in Christian communities and Christian cadres responsible for the work of typically political structures. This process erased lines of demarcation, and the initial alliance gradually developed into an integration. Suspicions came out into the open—and evaporated.

In their moral idealism, the revolutionaries weren't able to perceive how that moment, like a knife cutting into a stick of butter, had brought the class struggle to the heart of the Nicaraguan church. The presence of military chaplains in the National Guard was still dismissed as just a matter of a few priests corrupted by that decomposed society in which the excuse of living a comfortable life allowed basic moral principles to be forgotten.

HOPE AND FAITH IN TRYING CIRCUMSTANCES

Little by little hope was taking form in us that it would be possible to carry out a revolution with the full support of the [institutional] church on behalf of an afflicted and rebellious people. As we came to know selfless and intelligent men like Fernando Cardenal, the Jesuit priest who was destined to direct the National Literacy Crusade, our hopes grew apace. But history is stubborn as a Chontales mule, and the ideological representatives of resignation, exploitation, and death aligned themselves on the side of the rich and their imperial landlords.

That hope was a dream while we were dozing at the margin of history. We have now lost hope that certain leaders and sectors of the Nicaraguan church will take communion in the clay plates in which bread and nostalgia are scarce. But we have not lost hope in the eventual liberation of theology, which will be decisive for the plenary fulfillment of the theology of liberation.

In the midst of an often exasperating struggle, Christians continue to live a vital faith. Christians of humble background aim to live their faith in identification with their own class interests, and Christians originating in other social classes strive to be humble so as to identify with the poor—the poor who have ceased to be or are ceasing to be passive and obedient objects of the will of politicians and traditional religious leaders.

To these poor who, impelled by their situation, organize to seize lands in the countryside, or to secure prompt relief of problems in the cities, it proves difficult to believe that someone could identify with their economic misery without likewise identifying with their political needs and with their attitude in the face of the threatened return of a regime that was the cause of their poverty and repression. Nicaraguan Christians are learning not to modify their faith but to live it.

GRASPING THE REVOLUTIONARY MESSAGE OF THE BIBLE

Because we are not dogmatic, because we are steadfastly self-critical, the *Frente Sandinista* is a jealous guardian of our traditions. It is this antidogmatism that ultimately enabled us to mobilize the revolutionary force that Christians are capable of exercising. Father Gaspar García Laviana and the Christians who gave their lives for our revolution, and the Christians who today are ready to give their lives for the revolution, synthesize this experience.

The prophet Habakkuk had the Nicaraguan people before his eyes when he said [Hab. 1:3–4]: "Strife breaks out and altercations arise, because law disappears and righteousness is nowhere to be found. The unjust round up the just, so that justice is twisted." A revolution is precisely a dispute and an altercation that arises because law and righteousness have disappeared. To carry out a revolution is to straighten twisted justice, to shatter the chains of reactionary power with which the unjust shackle the just.

How are Christians who gained their education in the struggle of the poor to place themselves on the side of the rich, of whom the psalmist says, "they devour the needy and destitute"? How are they to put themselves on the side of those of whom Isaiah says [5:8]: "Woe unto those who accumulate house upon house and join field to field, until they occupy all the land and are left alone in the middle of the country"? The hour of the revolution is the hour when the rich remain alone; it's the hour of the sad alarms for those who have accumulated house upon house to begin the gnashing of teeth: "their stores have rotted and their garments are worm-eaten" [James 5:2].

The revolution is the tarnish the rich find on the gold and silver they accumulate; it's the fire that burns their flesh. Hell is none other than the clamor of wage earners, the groan of harvesters, the cry of the innocent who condemn because they hold the weapons of defense in their hands. Because as St. James says [1:9-11], "the rich will pass like the flower of the field. The sun rises, the heat mounts, the grass dries and the flower withers so that nothing remains of its beauty. Likewise the rich person will wither in the midst of his enterprises." The wealthy have withered in Nicaragua; we are helping them strip away their selfishness and we feel blessed to have so stripped them, so unrepentant and self-confident are they.

To be sure, the flower of the field doesn't dry out without resistance. Those who herded the poor, those who tortured justice, those who aggrandized and enriched themselves by filling their houses with what they obtained by fraud, those who did not respect the rights of the poor, those who fattened themselves and made a display of their possessions, those who set their eyes on fields and snatched them away, those who plotted wrongdoing in their beds and upon rising in the morning carried it out [Mic. 2:1-2], those who robbed houses instead of building them (Job points them out), those who believed that their gold and silver would never tarnish, those who thought the innocent would never begin to defend themselves, those who should be cast into the fire because they are trees that did not yield good fruit [Matt. 3:10, 7:15-20]—never in history have they resigned themselves to the loss of their power. They have always done everything possible to promote the triumphant return of the reign of decadence, injustice, and violence.

EXPERTS IN THE BUSINESS OF RELIGION

Already in the early days of Christianity Jesus himself, and before him prophets like Ezekiel, had to denounce those who tried to convert religion into "a commercial transaction." The classes our revolution dislodged from power were and are experts in the business of religion.

The illiteracy that for centuries devoured the creative capacity of our people is not alien to a particular type of religiosity that those classes know how to use with the same cleverness with which they extracted profits by tooth and nail. They fought the literacy campaign—through which in only four months we have succeeded in substantially reducing the illiteracy of centuries—by cynically arguing that we were forcibly tampering with the people's right to be ignorant.

But learning to read and write is barely the first step toward a critical and objective consciousness of the interrelationships among human beings and between them and nature. The formation of this consciousness is a process. This is why we have been so serious about establishing preschool centers, primary schools, and secondary schools throughout the country. But meanwhile certain attitudes, ideas, and habits persist, reinforced by repetition and ignorance across a span of almost five hundred years. Hence the opportunities for manipulation of the religious sentiments of the Nicaraguan people against its own revolution.

You have, by way of example, heard of the "sweating Virgin." The newspaper *La Prensa*—a U.S. daily published in Managua [applause]—gave it extensive publicity. This was a matter of a plaster statue that according to the propaganda was sweating for the sins of the revolution [laughter]. It was later discovered that the sweating was no more than an ordinary physical process, previously induced [by refrigerating the statue, then exposing it to the moist tropical air], and that *La Prensa* had been publicizing a fraud. In the same vein there was an attempt to make last year's floods seem like a punishment from God. And there's been an effort to portray religious figures as being persecuted by the government while promoting them as political figures. There's been a sustained campaign to try to provoke confrontation between the people and the revolutionary government, associating the latter with communism and associating religion with the defense of democracy and the U.S. way of life.

RELIGION IN COUNTERREVOLUTIONARY STRATEGY

As you know, this type of artificially created confrontation is encompassed within a broader strategy. Conscious of the revolutionary potential of Christianity, the enemies of humanity have recently begun to concede special strategic importance to the ideological struggle. This explains the formation of U.S. organizations like the Moral Majority, the Christian Voice, the Religious Round Table, and the Institute on Religion and Democracy, which I understand was visited by our illustrious archbishop of Managua. As is well known, the purpose of these organizations is to influence U.S. and Latin American churches.

Behind it all one finds the so-called East-West conflict. All our problems, if we accept this thesis, are derived from this conflict, so that in the particular case of Latin America the external enemy is the Soviet Union, Cuba, and Nicaragua, together with priests, ministers, and other Christians committed to the Nicaraguan revolution. All this has been made perfectly clear in the document produced by the Committee of Santa Fe and in the pronouncements of Reagan and his nostalgic group of advisers.

The Institute on Religion and Democracy is linked by various channels to the neoconservative movement that the Reagan administration in large measure reflects; among these is the Coalition for a Democratic Majority, created in 1972 and among whose membership stands out that distinguished lady, Jeane Kirkpatrick. It is significant that the IRD first appeared in 1981, and that it chose El Salvador for its first theme, announcing a campaign against the involvement of the churches in the Central American revolutionary process.

Under the guise of "democracy" and "reform," these groups seek a rollback policy to restore U.S. hegemony, giving priority to the struggle in the religious domain and in foreign policy, and unsuccessfully endeavoring to differentiate themselves from discredited conservative tendencies like McCarthyism and the "New Right," which emphasize the "internal enemy" and are formally more radical than the neoconservatism represented by the Reagan administration.

It is against this background that there was an attempt to provoke conflict under the guise of religion in August 1982 in the city of Masaya [when armed youths took over the Salesian school, then shot into a crowd of unarmed pro-Sandinista protesters, inflicting numerous casualties, including two deaths]. Here the counterrevolution tripped over the revolutionary faith of the Christian people.

This also explains the conflict they have tried to foment on the Atlantic coast by manipulating some Moravian and other pastors, and taking advantage of the ethnic and cultural differences of the Mískito population, artificially cultivated by the British in the period in which they tried to take over the Atlantic coast of Nicaragua, prefabricating a Mískito monarchy. Northern Zelaya, isolated by Mískito ethnicity, has sought to separate itself from Nicaragua by violence and terror. But Northern Zelaya is part of Nicaragua and any separatist intent is antihistorical, favoring only U.S. imperialism.

It is also against this background that one has to examine the misunderstandings that surrounded the recent papal visit to Nicaragua. It will be enough to cite one example to show to what point the merchants of religion went in trying to "sell" their wares, converting the figure of the pope into an advertisement. The day before the arrival of the pope, Somocista Guards [the *contras*] had murdered seventeen youths. The mothers of these youths pleaded with the pope for a prayer for their fallen children. The fragrance of martyrdom was still fresh to each of the five hundred thousand persons who had gathered to listen to the pope. Many of those in the Plaza 19 de Julio, who with tears in their eyes and with heart-rending cries requested a prayer for their deceased, were already aggrieved by the fact that their friends and relatives had fallen in defense of their country without the benefit of any prayer from the national ecclesiastical leadership. It was therefore understandable that upon encountering the person they considered God's highest representative, persons who for over forty years had been victims of violence should ask him to say a prayer for peace. No one can censure us if we mention this incident and deplore the lack of respect for the essentials of democracy, diplomacy, and good taste.

PERSECUTION

Under *somocismo*, there was religious persecution in Nicaragua. Priests and nuns were pursued and jailed, and some were assassinated. Persecution persists in some Central American countries. One can, for instance, find the murderer of Archbishop Oscar Romero among the functionaries of the current Salvadoran government.[5] Who doesn't know this? This is of course no fresh news item, and maybe for that reason the imperialist news media tell us nothing about religious persecution in El Salvador, whereas the

Prelate of the Counterrevolution [Cardinal Obando y Bravo] reiterates his reactionary political positions in public gatherings, sermons, homilies, and gossipy tales of the sacristy, citing the gospel out of context.

How, then, accuse the Sandinista revolution of religious persecution? It's easy. Let's apply Manichaeism and that's enough. The revolution is communist and therefore an enemy of religion. The priests who support the revolution must therefore have been duped and they've sold out to the gold of Moscow. Our historical commitment to respect and strengthen the religious content of the feasts of patron saints is a sham, as are the tears we shed at the death of Archbishop Romero. . . . We haven't assassinated priests, but that is but a tactical maneuver [laughter]. That we haven't closed churches is surely to fool public opinion. We received the pope and spent tens of millions of cordobas in transportation and courtesies but, clearly, it was only to insult him by asking that he pray for our dead and for peace.

Why is it, I wonder, that many Christians have been accused of being Marxists and never has a Marxist been accused of being a Christian? [laughter and applause].

What is actually happening? Monsignor José Arias Caldera and Dominican priest Manuel Batalla have been removed from their parishes, and U.S. Jesuit Peter Marchetti and Spanish Jesuit Luis Medrano have been suspended from offering Mass, to cite but a few of the pressures that have had to be borne by many of the clergy. Who, then, is the persecutor? Who are the persecuted? In accord with the gospel of imperialism, identifying with the poor is anti-Christian and identifying with U.S. foreign policy is observance of the commandments of the law of God [applause].

In Latin America the persecuted priests, monks, and nuns have always been those who identified themselves with the poor—persecuted in Chile, persecuted in El Salvador, persecuted in Honduras, and persecuted in Nicaragua for the same reason. But we are not the persecutors. That is why Bishop Romero said: "In America the church suffers the fate of the poor: persecution." And like the fate of the poor is the fate of the Nicaraguan revolution: the Nicaraguan revolution is persecuted, just as Christians are persecuted.

THE BEAST AND CAIAPHAS

In Latin America 40 percent of the population lives in rags, with empty stomachs. It is not precisely known whether illiteracy reaches 40 or 60 or 70 percent of the Central American population. Of each thousand infants born, more than two hundred are victims of homicide—above all by gastroenteritis—without being known to the tribunals of justice.

The merchants of counterrevolutions will be able to so contrive things that these contradictions advance toward explosion at a turtle's pace, but they will not be able to prevent the final fuse from being ignited one of these days, which will set the Latin American dust ablaze.

In Nicaragua they have interfered with our external sources of financing, but they will not be able to exhaust the sources of popular creativity. Imperialism has the very real capacity to reduce our foreign exchange to the point of driving us to anger and self-pity, but it will be incapable of exhausting our reserves of patriotism, our will to resist. The counterrevolution will go on destroying roads, schools, and day-care centers, but it will not be able to prevent our recently literate peasants from continuing to acquire the perspectives of the literate. . . .

The beast will continue to buy out Caiaphases, but will not be able to buy out Nicaraguan Christians so that they cease being revolutionaries [applause].

NO TO THE LIONS

In Nicaragua we have [by an August 1980 law] prohibited the use of religious symbols in commercial advertising, which had become a Christmastime custom for selling imported clothes and illusions. In Nicaragua we have said no to the lions who devour humans for the delight of magnates; and as seriously as we strive for the multiplication of the loaves, we are averse to the idiotic, ridiculous, and homogenizing market of superfluous consumption.

The possibilities for economic development are objectively limited. Although we have succeeded in ameliorating misery, we will remain poor in the foreseeable future. For the time being our only possible option is the resurrection of life—that is to say, the embodiment of love. And to achieve this aim we are prosecuting selfishness in the tribunal of life and love. We are going to bring an end to egotism and divisiveness. Though it should cost us excommunication or death, we are going to build the communitarian society that was conceived, though in elemental terms, by the first Christians in the Roman catacombs—with a clear understanding of new economic and social dimensions.

This is not easy. We inherited a dependent society, with rat holes and contaminated waters. The Nicaraguan economy struggles tooth and nail for autonomous development, confronting inflexible control mechanisms of the international market, technological monopolies, and the denial of financing. Remnants of precapitalist production, which maintain salaries at substantially lower levels than the real value of labor, will persist for some time. Nicaragua, the land of the resurrection of the living, is fenced in by military aggression, foreign debt, and the penetrating fangs of unjust terms of trade. . . .

DEFENDING THE POSSIBILITY OF PEACE

We have but one option: to defend ourselves—defend ourselves from criminal guns and lying and criminal teletypes. We are going to defend our social transformations; we are going to defend our right to be in charge of our own decisions; we are going to defend peace and the search for peace.

The Sandinista revolution has certainly awakened contradictions across Central America; it has changed the rules of the game between oppressors and oppressed. But from these contradictions will emerge a synthesis that will pass by way of liberation to lead to a definitive peace in Central America. We are the vanguard of peace, and for this reason we are hated by those who have made of war their preferred instrument of domination, their raison d'être.

We must organize our defense. If we were to fail to do so, with what weapons would we confront death and defend life? With what weapons would we defend the possibility of peace?

Our army was created to defend peace. It is not an army to launch aggression against other peoples, but to defend Nicaragua. The traditional armies that dominate much of Latin America are armies of aggression against their own peoples. Our army will never be able to carry out aggression against the Nicaraguan people, because our army *is* the Nicaraguan people.

Our weapons defend the survival of our children; they defend the alphabet conquered by our people; they defend the land we've turned over to the *campesinos*; they defend the strategic objective of a new morality.

The U.S. government decided, in the name of "God and democracy," to be the master of our decisions, and it now becomes savagely irritated when it perceives that we have placed ourselves between its eyebrows, imitating the example of David [when he slew Goliath]. Its officials will not forgive us for snatching the profaned communion breads from their teeth, and we commit the unpardonable folly of believing that [in the words of Sandino] the sovereignty of a people is not to be discussed but defended with weapons in hand [applause].

A NEW SYNTHESIS

I will not speak of our errors or inexperience, so that you will not think we are pessimists; on the contrary, we shall move forward, we shall survive, and we shall triumph.

You have engaged in theological reflection on liberation and peace from the perspective of the poor. With faith enough to meet any test, we believe in the philosophy of liberation and in the exodus from misery to take on the problem of poverty. Afterward will come new stages of development whose principal wealth lies in the work to satisfy the fundamental needs of human beings and society, where extravagance and the expropriation of the work of some by others is forbidden.

Perhaps someday we will join our dearly loved Christian friends and brothers in adopting the philosophy of Christianity. For the time being, we reiterate with you our communion of love for the poor, our identification with the humble, our exclusive preference for the poor.

We do not renounce, we will never renounce, our commitment to life, to happiness, to a society of human fellowship, where the moral principles of the revolution and the moral principles of Christianity come together so as to enter into a synthesis that goes beyond orthodoxy and formalized logic. In spite of everything, it is still possible to reject involution, to come together beyond dogmas, and finally to discover that human beings are vulnerable to love.

NOTES

1. The *Iglesia de Candelaria* was destroyed by the 1972 Managua earthquake. In an interview with Mexican journalist Gregorio Selser published in *Barricada* on January 8, 1986 (p. 3), Borge pointed out that a *somocista* uncle of his, Bishop Carlos Borge y Castrillo, was among those who designated Somoza a "prince of the church."

2. "Neighbor" is rendered *prójimo* ("fellow being") in Spanish, akin to *próximo* ("next one"), as in the parable of the good Samaritan.

3. This is at least in part a reference to Pope John Paul II's response to such entreaties from the multitudes during his 1983 visit to Nicaragua.

4. St. Hilary of Poitiers (c. A.D. 315–367), theologian, elected bishop of Poitiers c. 353.

5. Major Roberto D'Aubuisson, who was then president of the Salvadoran legislature, has been reported (e.g., by former U.S. ambassador Robert White) to have masterminded the assassination of Archbishop Romero, with former Nicaraguan National Guard Lt. Col. (and more recently FDN *contra* counterintelligence chief) Ricardo Lau as the paid hitman.

13

Letter to Father Uriel Molina
(1984)

This letter was written on July 3, 1984, on the occasion of Uriel Molina's 25th anniversary in the priesthood.

Just as Ernesto Cardenal was an early leader in developing rural Christian opposition to the Somoza regime, Uriel Molina was an early leader in developing its urban counterpart. In the early 1970s, a group of students at the Jesuit-run University of Central America who were seeking concrete expression of the "preferential option for the poor" moved in with Father Molina in Managua's lower-class Barrio Riguero. The Christian community that grew out of this experience was to play a catalytic role in the revolution. Alumni Luis Carrión and Joaquín Cuadra are among those who became major Sandinista figures, and the barrio as a whole was a center of insurrectionary activity during the fight to topple Somoza.

Following the July 1979 revolutionary triumph, Father Molina founded the Antonio Valdivieso Ecumenical Center in Managua, named after a bishop martyred in 1550 for his defense of Nicaraguan indigenous peoples against an earlier set of tyrants (the Contreras). The center, in which Catholics and Protestants work side by side (a Protestant minister co-directs the center with Molina), is one of Nicaragua's foremost institutions devoted to the study and practice of liberation theology.

Managua, July 3, 1984

Father Uriel Molina
Managua

Uriel:

I remember our first encounters in the dark days of December, during our childhood, and common journeys beneath the splendid sun of Holy Week, when we participated in the opening chapter of a Christian faith that, acknowledging the words of Jesus Christ, dismissed the cruelty of hell as incompatible with the infinite generosity of God. Afterward, each of us followed the path of different disciplines and geographies. Each of us—like many other young persons—fought for the heirs of those humble workers who joined together in the desert and on the banks of the Jordan with the young and rebellious preacher who in the ninth hour was crucified by the dominant classes of the time.

The struggle brought us, over the years, to the same stage of

Borge with Father Uriel Molina in the latter's church of
San Francisco de los Angeles, Barrio Riguero, Managua

"The obligatory simplicity of your life grants you that spiritual plenitude we all envy."

identity with the poor, though each from the vantage point of his own calling.

If we were to make balance sheets of our lives, beloved brother, I believe yours has been more full and whole.

In my life there's gunpowder, inflamed multitudes, official receptions, unavoidable protocols, certain bitternesses that render more detectable the indescribable tastes of duty fulfilled. . . .

Your exemplary life of everyday identification with the poor, those who surround your parish with psalms and hopes, is not foreign to the heritage of Franciscan humility, that if you think about it, isn't much different from what revolutionary humility should be. We are not always—at least from the standpoint of my own life—sufficiently devoted to this ideal.

The obligatory simplicity of your life, accepted by you with cheerfulness, grants you precisely that spiritual plenitude we all envy.

Twenty-five years of spiritual life, of sorrows and hopes shared with your community, come together in moments like those in which Luis, Joaquín, and Javier searched out the path of combat to the popular triumph passing by the waystation of your parish;[1] in your clandestine contacts; in the valiant words of Masses and in joyful, stimulating processions, full of enthusiasm and faith in God and the revolution; in the prudent and inevitable confrontation with the nostalgias of the night.

These few words, Father Uriel, my friend, are to be added to the many that have been showered on you with justified fondness, so that at least you should be completely assured that your pastoral labor has won our admiration and respect.

Fraternally,
Tomás Borge

NOTE

1. Luis Carrión is today vice-minister of the interior, as well as one of the *Comandantes de la Revolución* who make up the National Directorate of the FSLN. Joaquín Cuadra is vice-minister of defense and chief of staff of the armed forces. Javier Carrión (a cousin of Luis) is now FSLN political delegate for the sixth region (Boaco and Chontales).

14

Nicaragua: Resurrected and Not to Be Crucified Anew
(1985)

In the spring of 1985, Nicaragua found itself under simultaneous assault by the Empire and the Vatican. In April the Vatican announced the elevation of the revolution's prime domestic opponent—Archbishop Miguel Obando y Bravo—to the status of cardinal. Following his investiture in Rome, Cardinal Obando went on to Miami to celebrate Mass among counterrevolutionaries and stalwarts of the old Somoza regime. He then returned to Nicaragua, where in the course of exhibiting his new red robes throughout the country he reiterated his message that peace would come only through "dialogue" with the armed counterrevolution.

On May 1, President Reagan's economic blockade of Nicaragua went into effect, striking yet another blow at the economy of a small, poor country already straining under the burden of war. This measure was soon followed by the U.S. Congress' approval of the president's request for $27 million in "humanitarian" aid to the contras.

Tomás Borge responded to these developments in the light of Christian faith and Sandinista principles in the closing address of the Sixth Continental Assembly of the World Federation of Christian Student Movements, held at the Managua headquarters of the Nicaraguan Baptist Convention on June 15, 1985.

We have listened with profound respect to your presentations as delegates of the World Federation of Christian Student Movements, representing as you do numerous countries of Latin America, Europe, and the United States. Like you we have been moved by the shocking record of victims of the counterrevolution: the one hundred fifty murdered children, the additional sixty-five hundred who have been orphaned, the nine hundred schools that have been destroyed, the nine thousand murdered *campesinos,* and all the other statistics that reveal the underlying philosophy of the U.S. government. If this gathering is centered on Jesus' saying that "I've come so that you may have life and have it in abundance [John 10:10]," we could say that Mr. Reagan has come that we might have death and have it in abundance.

A FEDERATION TRUE TO ITS FAITH

It does not surprise me that the World Federation of Christian Student Movements decided to hold its Sixth Continental Assembly here in Managua, in view of your support for our country and your denunciation of the economic blockade that has been imposed on us with blood, fire, and tears.

Not everyone may know of this federation that has supplied leaders to the World Council of Churches, that has distinguished itself in the struggle against fascism and racism, that has supported the liberation struggles of African and Latin American peoples, that has given rise to figures of global prominence such as Nobel Peace Prize recipient Bishop Desmond Tutu, and, here in Latin America, to persons like Methodist minister Emilio Castro, who after being expelled from Uruguay by the military dictatorship has shared the hardships of the diaspora with his exiled people.

From the time of its foundation at the end of the nineteenth century, this federation has defended its faith rooted in the fundamental principle that "they will be known by their fruits [Matt. 7:16]," but above all that the fruits by which Christians—and I would add, all human beings—will be recognized and judged are social in nature and imply that the practice of Christian faith (and of the good conscience of those who are not Christians) is at the same time the practice of a commitment to the aspirations of freedom and justice of the oppressed.

You, the representatives of this federation, believe in a God whom the psalmist describes as liberating the poor from the powerful. Who are the powerful and who are the poor? Who were the ones who throughout our history despoiled us of wealth, sovereignty, independence, and dignity, submitting us to underdevelopment beneath the vigilance of overseers they now wish to restore out of nostalgia for the past?

How could you not be alongside us in such circumstances? For as the psalmist says: "The poor find refuge in you, you succor the orphan, and break the arm of the unjust and the wicked" [see Ps. 37:11-17]. How could you not be alongside the poor and the orphans of Nicaragua, now that the unjust and the wicked lift their arm against them? How could you not be alongside those who cry out for the fulfillment of justice demanded by the Bible through all its prophets? How could you not join the struggle to stop that menacing arm, in company with a revolution that in acting against local and international oppressors fulfills the Book of Job's prophecies against the rich: "Their children will have to pay back the poor, their hands will have to return their wealth [20:10]"?

How, in this moment when U.S. imperialism is redoubling its aggression, can we not expect the enthusiastic support of this federation, of the U.S. and Canadian National Council of Churches, of the World Council of Churches, and of all truly observant Christians whose faith, though postulating that its kingdom is of another world, at the same time demands a this-worldly commitment to those who hunger and thirst for justice?

It likewise does not surprise me that those who traffic in the sweat and blood of whole peoples turn the Christian religion into a falsified hallmark that allows their lies to pass for truths, their despoliation and robbery for generosity, their defense of oppression for defense of freedom, their aggression against the people for liberation, their nostalgia for the dictatorship that exploited this people for democracy. But they have come to be known by their works. Their talent for disguise is that of the Iscariot kissing the cheek of the betrayed, that of the tearing of garments to confound the people, the judgment that instead of calling for the punishment of the oppressor calls for the punishment of the oppressed, and instead of asking that the arm of the unjust be stayed, asks the just to disarm and submit.

SANDINISTA FLEXIBILITY AND FIRMNESS

Who, Christian *compañeros,* can accuse us of intransigence? If there's anything this revolution can be accused of it is indulgence, at times to the point of exhaustion, at times to the point of renouncing some of our legitimate rights.

The yearning for peace expressed by Cardinal Obando in yesterday's prudent homily is completely understandable. And in fact we have thoroughly explored the road to peace, turning it into the communion of our secular rites. . . .

Let it not be said we're the ones who don't want peace. Yesterday, on Cardinal Obando's return to Nicaragua amid the jubilation of many Christians, groups of instigators attacked the police. We had decided to disarm the police, leading to the curious phenomenon that instead of a repressive police, we find in Nicaragua a police repressed by small groups of provocateurs, previously organized by persons connected with those who arranged the cardinal's welcoming ceremonies. We know from a number of sources of the involvement of certain representatives of the counterrevolution and of reactionary political parties, both following directives laid out by the U.S. embassy. . . .

In truth, we are very prudent and careful, and there will never be a repressive police force here. But let it not be thought that we will allow yesterday's vandalism, and the wounding of many of the police who patiently endured the provocations, to become established as a routine. Yesterday's events do not constitute any precedent; we will not permit the violation of revolutionary legality, the abuse of revolutionary patience, through further attacks on the police.

A SINISTER GAME OF MIRRORS

It should hardly be necessary to say we are something more than mere partisans of concord, of peace. Our opponents are practically shoving their fingers in our eyes, accusing us of being totalitarians, and demanding something we in fact insisted on ourselves: to hold elections. And besides their underhanded and futile maneuvers designed to rob the November 1984 elections of legitimacy in the court of world opinion, they continue to accuse us of being totalitarian, as if absolutely nothing had happened in this country.

As in a sinister game of mirrors, they reiterate the accusation that Nicaragua isn't interested in peaceful solutions in Central America. And this despite the fact that we shattered the glass that reflected this image when we became the only ones to agree to sign the Contadora Treaty that set forth concrete solutions and mutual concessions.[1] But the sinister mirrors have been pieced together again, and we continue to be the "enemies of peace" in Central America.

The echoes of these lies rebound through their television networks and the front pages of their newspapers. They claim we have subverted our neighbors, sending men, guns, and bombs to El Salvador, and building a powerful army that threatens defenseless Costa Rica and peaceful Honduras. All this even though it is *we* who have proposed the establishment of demilitarized zones under international supervision. It's as if we hadn't said a word.

We continue to be a base of aggression against these sibling countries. Never mind that it's not in Nicaragua but in Honduras that all those ostentatious military maneuvers with tanks, infantry, warplanes, naval forces, and communications media are carried out. Never mind that it isn't in Honduras or Costa Rica but in Nicaragua that thousands of men and women, children and the elderly, are dying. *We* are shedding the blood, but we're the aggressors. Our mothers are the .ones shedding tears, yet *we* are the victimizers. Our modest means of production and our social services are the ones being destroyed, but *we* are quite simply the ravaging bandits. Counterrevolutionary armies are organized on Honduran and Costa Rican territory, but *we* are the aggressors. Though *they* prepare the guillotine, the gallows, and the firing squad for Nicaraguans, it is *we* who are the executioners.

They also accuse us of not wanting dialogue. Yet we have engaged in dialogue with the Catholic hierarchy, with whom we believe it's possible to maintain a relationship of mutual respect. And we have also engaged in dialogue with the progenitor of our thousand injuries at Manzanillo,[2] and have insisted by every synonym in the dictionary that we are prepared to resume it. Manzanillo has by now come to symbolize the intransigence of the arrogant and all-powerful *señor.*[3]

We have engaged in dialogue with groups along the Atlantic coast that have taken up arms against the revolution. We very much hope to continue our talks with MISURASATA and its leader

Brooklyn Rivera, especially because some of the rights they are claiming are just and are supported by the FSLN.[4] We are interested in dialogue with Brooklyn Rivera because he is neither a *somocista* nor a traitor, even if he has been using mistaken methods very costly to both his people and the rest of us Nicaraguans.

The autonomy process for the Atlantic coast is an important step in the search for a solution to the conflict there.[5] It will surely facilitate future dialogue with various sectors with whom there has been mutual misunderstanding, sectors that are neither *somocista* nor traitorous, but are Nicaraguans who have become confused in a cultural misunderstanding that the imperialists are taking advantage of to recruit cannon fodder.

Borge with Reverend Jesse Jackson

"We have turned the road to peace into the communion of our secular rites."

Who can say we are inflexible, that we reject dialogue? Who can think we don't want a negotiated settlement to the Central American conflict? Wasn't it the Sandinista Popular Revolution that unilaterally decided to cancel the introduction of new arms systems and withdraw foreign advisers, without any corresponding move from the other side?

All these initiatives have been shattered on a wall of silence. They have been consumed by visceral hatred, by the irrationality of Mr. Reagan who, while invoking God, has decided to destroy Nicaragua. The ears of the Reagan administration delight only in the sound of cannons and warships; the Reagan administration is deafer than an adobe wall when it comes to listening to prayers for peace, the inconsolable weeping of mothers, the unswerving resonance of our national dignity.

RESURRECTION: NOT TO BE RENOUNCED

Tell us, Christians, what is left for us to do? We have turned the other cheek more than a dozen times. We have been crucified repeatedly, having been sacrificed in 1856, again in 1912, and again in 1926, after which they imposed Satan himself on us.[6] What is left for us to do? What is our duty? To keep on turning the other cheek? To go on being crucified? We have emerged from the tomb, the third day has already arrived for the Nicaraguan people, and it has arrived forever [prolonged applause].

The only option we have left is to defend our resurrection. To defend our triumphant rebirth we cannot disarm ourselves while spears, hammers, and nails are being readied under our very noses, while they have contingency plans to invade us, plans to reduce their embassy staff and then break diplomatic relations—and don't ask how we know about this [laughter] because we have friends all over, even in the heart of the beast.

They are planning to train about one hundred twenty-five thousand men, about sixty-five thousand of whom would be combat troops. They have figured out the numbers of warplanes, helicopters, doctors, and paramedics they will need. And they have even calculated the number of casualties they will sustain, speaking of some three thousand in the first month. At any rate I think we should more thoroughly prepare ourselves so that these calculations don't go beyond being hypothetical figures pulled out of computers, because there is no doubt that we and they alike would pay a high price. As much as it pains us to contemplate the deaths on both sides, we'd inflict as many casualties as we'd be able to.

We do not want to be sacrificed again. We do not and will not renounce the resurrection, just as we do not and will not renounce dialogue—but dialogue that involves mutual concessions, not capitulation. We will renounce defense once defense is unnecessary, for no one sets aside the shield while surrounded by daggers. We will renounce the solidarity of foreign advisers once the cause that gave rise to them disappears, for no one turns away the friendly hand while at the edge of the abyss.

A HYPOCRITICAL DECLARATION OF WAR

Not only has the U.S. government rejected dialogue, but it has persistently widened the field and escalated the intensity of its aggression: unilaterally suspending credits, blocking sources of international financing, forming a counterrevolutionary army that specializes in crushing skulls and corrupting souls, suspending our sugar quota, mining our harbors, mounting an economic blockade, violating our airspace and territorial waters, sending troops on offensive maneuvers along our border, lying and slandering to misrepresent all this, and showing contempt for the views of its own people as well as those of the international community.

They accuse us of banditry as they put the pistol to our chest with the intention of robbing us of our dignity because they cannot hope to rob us of our heart. For we have turned our heart over to all the peoples of the world. Our Nicaraguan heart belongs to humanity, and will never be made to kneel before U.S. imperialism [applause].

They are now legalizing their financing of the counterrevolution. A majority of their Congress has decided to legalize illegality, legalizing aggression against Nicaragua in the context of an undeniable violation of international law, manifesting a dangerous contempt for humankind and for all the international institutions created in recent years.

Who gives one country's Congress the right to designate millions of dollars for the murder of citizens of another country? Something that would be unthinkable in Europe seems almost normal in the U.S.A—the right of the powerful to determine the destiny of a small country. Such a hypocritical declaration of war, such an institutionalization of the mentality of Judas and the devil, has no place in the mind of honorable human beings.

DIALOGUE WITH THE COUNTERREVOLUTION?

What is their conditon for ceasing their aggression? They want us to engage in dialogue with the counterrevolution. This is supposed to be the magic formula that would end the war and bring peace to Nicaragua. But what peace are they talking about? What would it mean to engage in dialogue with the counterrevolution? It would mean engaging in dialogue with those who massacred our people over decades, criminals like ex-National Guardsman [and current *contra* commander-in-chief] Enrique Bermúdez. It would mean sitting at the negotiating table with those who bombed Estelí, León, Matagalpa, and Masaya; with those who murdered the Indians of Monimbó and Subtiava. . . .

How could we discuss the interests of Nicaraguan workers with those who murdered longshoremen, bus drivers, teachers, construction workers, students, and nurses in response to their efforts to secure their rights? How could we converse with those who only three days ago attacked a peasant settlement, murdering and destroying, raping women, burning sixty-one houses, and leaving another twenty children orphaned? What would it mean to negotiate with the counterrevolution? It would mean negotiating the land we have turned over to the *campesinos,* reversing the Agrarian Reform. This is exactly what happened after the assassination of Sandino, when they seized the lands Sandino had turned over to cooperatives, restoring them to the landlords. It would also mean discussing the disarmament of the people, just as the *campesinos* of Las Segovias were disarmed after the assassination of Sandino.

But in the last analysis, who is harmed by our people in arms? Who, apart from enemies of the people, is harmed by our having handed out weapons to the people? Because if Nicaraguans should not want this revolution, they have but to realign the sights on their rifles to overthrow the government. Yet these rifles in the hands of the people are actually strengthening the government. This flies in the face of those who say we have lost popular support. Could this armed people invade defenseless Costa Rica or peaceful Honduras? Theoretically, hundreds of thousands of Nicaraguans could undertake such a feat, but it would go against our principles—and beyond that, against common sense. For isn't the U.S.A. looking for some hair in the soup, some pretext to invade us? Suppose we should be so crazy as to move into Honduras and seize Choluteca, or into Costa Rica and take Liberia. Wouldn't the U.S. Marines immediately descend on Central America? Which is exactly what we're trying to avoid. So apart from the fact that we would not do it for the fundamental reason that we respect international law, we could not do it for political and military reasons. We have no warplanes, submarines, or sophisticated weapons systems, so that it is impossible for us to threaten Central America. And yet we're a danger to the national security of the United States!

But all right, to engage in dialogue with the counterrevolution would also mean negotiating the dissolution of organizations of workers, peasants, students, women, and children, as happened in the period when they dissolved the peasant cooperatives on the Río Coco and the nascent labor movement led by that extraordinary organizer Berta Munguía. Their idea of dialogue entails holding new elections, eliminating the Sandinista Defense Committees, eliminating State Security, eliminating the Sandinista Armed Forces, eliminating the Sandinista Police. Those who make such a proposal are completely crazy and anyone who would accept it is even crazier, and I can assure you we are quite sane [applause].

OPEN ARMS TO ALL WHO HAVE SINNED

Of course we do not rule out internal dialogue, and we are ready to accept the reincorporation of counterrevolutionaries into society, regardless of the rank they hold in the counterrevolutionary forces. It is no accident that we've accepted the return of former National Guardsman and *contra* Regional Task Force Commander Oswaldo Mondragón, who is in complete freedom despite the fact that if we were to assess his conduct by the law, he would have to be imprisoned. This revolution opens its arms to all who have sinned, absolving all who want to return. As we have said on other occasions, we are not interested in destroying sinners, but rather in ending sin once and for all.

History, on the other hand, has taught us what it means to negotiate with the Moncadas, Díazes, and Somozas, whose rotting hearts continue to beat in the chests of Calero, Bermúdez, and the traitor Pastora.[7] They negotiated with Sandino in order to murder him, and now they want to negotiate with the revolution in order to murder it as well. They negotiated with Sandino in order to massacre the pesants of Wiwilí, in order to repress workers, in order to surrender our natural resources to the Empire. They negotiated with Sandino, and it was from those negotiations that the long and sinister night of *somocismo* emerged. Those who today demand these inconceivable negotiations would like to have history repeat itself, but they forget that history never repeats itself once its teachings are assimilated.

The National Guard was created and sustained by the U.S. Marines; Somoza was the last of these Marines. Now they have rebaptized this *somocista* Guard, calling it the FDN [Nicaraguan Democratic Force], and preparing it to once again act as an extension of the U.S. armed forces. To negotiate with such puppets would be to accept that the U.S.A has the right to decide Nicaragua's destiny, to resign ourselves to a false sovereignty. We wouldn't be negotiating; we would be kneeling, betraying our principles. We are ready to resume the Manzanillo talks with the United States—that is to say, with the puppeteer who pulls the strings, but we will never negotiate our sovereignty either in Manzanillo or anywhere else.

Dear friends, we have a proven dedication to understanding, negotiation, reasonable solutions, mutual concessions. We have given and given, but don't ask any more of us without reciprocity. We need peace like fish need water and birds need open spaces in which to fly. But peace is one thing and submission another. Peace is to us like maize, but liberty is like the air we breathe. If peace is to us as the countryside, liberty is like light. Dear friends, we love peace as much as we love life, but we love the freedom of this country even more than we love life.

That's why we say: a free homeland or death! [sustained applause].

NOTES

1. The Contadora Group (named after the Panamanian island where it first met) represents four Latin American countries—Mexico, Panama, Venezuela, and Colombia—that have embarked on a precedent-setting regional initiative to head off the U.S. drift into a Central American war. The first product of this venture was a September 1984 draft treaty

prohibiting foreign military bases, maneuvers, and advisers, limiting weapons systems, and forbidding transfers of weapons to insurgents throughout Central America. When Nicaragua agreed to sign the treaty, the U.S.A. prevailed on El Salvador, Honduras, and Costa Rica (all heavily dependent on U.S. aid) to block the treaty. With the Contadora process jeopardized, four other Latin American countries (Brazil, Peru, Argentina, and Uruguay) joined in, establishing the first pan-Latin challenge to the U.S. traditional "Monroe Doctrine" domination of Latin America.

2. Manzanillo is the Mexican city in which the governments of the United States and Nicaragua held bilateral talks in 1984, until the United States walked out to pursue its efforts to overthrow the Nicaraguan government by force of arms.

3. *Señor* is no longer in usage in revolutionary Nicaragua, as it is a holdover from feudal forms of address. Its usage in this instance is not a form of politeness but a sarcastic reference to the feudal lord in Washington.

4. MISURASATA was born of an effort to organize the indigenous peoples of Nicaragua's Caribbean flank after the revolutionary triumph of July 19, 1979. The name is an acronym for "Miskito, Sumu, Rama, and Sandinista Together," symbolizing a cooperative intent that rapidly fell apart. The Sandinistas were initially insensitive to regional perspectives, trying to extend formulas derived from the experience of the Pacific slope of the continental divide to the very different realities of the Caribbean slope. For its part, MISURASATA laid claim to one-third of Nicaragua's land mass on behalf of one-twentieth of its population, on the basis of "aboriginal rights." The situation degenerated into armed conflict, with Brooklyn Rivera leading MISURASATA guerrilla forces from Costa Rican headquarters, and Steadman Fagoth leading rival MISURA forces (allied with the FDN *contras)* out of Honduran camps. In late 1984, the government entered into peace talks with MISURASATA that broke down in 1985. The government has since negotiated local cease-fires with Miskito field commanders.

5. Despite the breakdown in the MISURASATA talks, the Sandinistas have set in motion an Autonomy Process intended to formally recognize the cultural, religious, linguistic, and land tenure rights of the peoples of the Caribbean region of the country, and to draft a constitutional provision for the establishment of two regional governments (one for the northeast, the other for the southeast) consisting of freely-elected legislatures empowered to set regional policies in accord with cultural priorities, and to appoint regional administrators.

6. In 1855 William Walker, a Tennesseean, led a force of U.S. freebooters who seized control of Nicaragua. Proclaiming himself president, he

reinstated slavery, and was promptly recognized by U.S. President Franklin Pierce, a northern "doughface" ally of southerners seeking new slave states to counter free-state gains in the Senate. Walker was eventually defeated and executed in Honduras (in 1857) after he tried to take over all of Central America.

In 1909 nationalist President José Santos Zelaya, who was interested in developing a second isthmian canal, through Lake Nicaragua, was pressured out of office by U.S. Secretary of State Philander Knox, who fomented a Conservative revolt for the purpose. To forestall a nationalist victory in the ensuing civil war, President Taft sent in the U.S. Marines in 1912. Nationalist forces under General Benjamín Zeledón made a valiant stand outside Masaya, but were no match for the invasion force, and Zeledón was slain before the year was out. The U.S.A. then installed Adolfo Díaz, a pliant chief accountant of a U.S. mining firm (whose counsel happened to have been Philander Knox himself), in the presidency.

U.S. Marines again invaded in 1926, when the Coolidge administration became disturbed by what it perceived as an over-independent attitude on the part of President Juan Bautista Sacasa. He was replaced with the ever-trustworthy Adolfo Díaz, who obediently made a formal request for further U.S. intervention in Nicaragua's domestic affairs. It was against this intervention that Augusto Sandino launched his successful guerrilla war against the U.S. Marines. The Marines withdrew in 1933, but not before creating the National Guard as an extension of U.S. influence. It was but a year later that Sandino was assassinated on the orders of National Guard commander Anastasio Somoza García, who later installed himself as president through a coup d'état.

7. General José María Moncada initially led the Liberal forces against the U.S.-installed Díaz government in 1926 (see preceding note), but entered into a deal with U.S. Secretary of State Henry Stimson at Tipitapa in 1927 by which he was to be enabled to gain the presidency in 1930 in return for disbanding his troops. It was left to General Augusto Sandino to carry on the struggle for national sovereignty.

Enrique Bermúdez, a former colonel in Somoza's National Guard, is military commander of the main *contra* force, the *Fuerza Democrática Nicaragüense,* based in Honduras. Former Nicaraguan Coca-Cola executive and CIA operative Adolfo Calero is the top civilian figure in the FDN. Former Sandinista Edén Pastora formed a competing *contra* group based in Costa Rica, but has recently abandoned his efforts as a result of military reverses and CIA intrigues against him for his unwillingness to join forces with ex-*somocistas.*

15

Autonomy for the Atlantic Coast (1986)

One of the most controversial aspects of the Nicaraguan revolution has been its treatment of ethnic minorities—particularly the Miskito Amerindians—on the Caribbean side of the country, commonly known as the Atlantic Coast. Though there are many elements of truth in the accusations of maltreatment that have been leveled against the Sandinistas, they have become lost in a sea of distortions, exaggerations, and outright fabrications propagated by the Reagan administration to serve its propaganda war against Managua. A case in point is the oft-repeated charge of genocide. The objective base for this accusation consists of the murders (some documented, others probable) of about one hundred Miskito prisoners at Leimus and other locations by Sandinista forces in 1981 and 1982. What has generally gone unreported is that (1) the Leimus murders may have been carried out in response to similar murders of Sandinista prisoners at San Carlos a week earlier; (2) local Sandinista units appear to have acted without the knowledge or approval of the Sandinista leadership; (3) many of those responsible for atrocities have been sentenced to prison terms; and (4) no further atrocities have been documented since 1982. To this it should be added that the Sandinistas have freed all Atlantic Coast prisoners through general amnesties in 1983, 1985, and 1986.

In nearby Guatemala, on the other hand, the numbers of Mayan Amerindians slaughtered by government forces during the same

149

period runs into the tens of thousands, with no sign of relief, and no possibility of punishment for those responsible. To single out the Sandinistas for condemnation is therefore pure hypocrisy. And now that the Sandinistas have publicly acknowledged their errors, and have acted to correct them, the only genuinely Christian response to their repentance is forgiveness.

A new chapter in the Sandinista relationship with the inhabitants of the Caribbean Coast was opened in the spring of 1985, when Tomás Borge was assigned responsibility for the Atlantic Coast by the National Directorate of the FSLN. By summer, Borge had given permission to Miskitos who had earlier been removed far inland from their villages along the Coco River (in a war zone on the Honduran border) to return to their homes. Most significantly, he then announced the initiation of a process of autonomy designed to secure ethnic and linguistic rights, and institute regional self-government for the inhabitants of the Atlantic Coast. Here, in the opening address to the Symposium on Autonomy held at the César Augusto Silvio Convention Center in Managua on July 13, 1986, Borge outlines the new Sandinista understanding of ethnic rights and autonomy that has gradually emerged out of the experience of the preceding seven years. As usual, Borge's presentation is salted with Christian values and allusions even when, as in this case, he is not addressing a Christian gathering (many of the invited guests were non-Christian Amerindians).

Allow me, dear *compañeros,* to share the rejoicing of over one hundred delegates and numerous guests invited to this symposium. . . . We welcome our brother, Bishop Sergio Méndez Arceo [of Cuernavaca, Mexico], who has come to Nicaragua to attend both this symposium and the Nineteenth of July [seventh anniversary celebration of the revolution]. . . .

THE MASSACRE OF 1934

In the 1940s, some Moravian pastors recorded the oral tradition of a Miskito community. The tradition tells of a massacre of Miskitos and Sumus along the banks of the Wanki River in the early summer of 1934, as they constructed an agricultural cooperative and dreamed of peace. The bodies of the Amerindians were thrown into the river, which, like a native divinity, dissolved them in its waters and led them to sea. As the Miskitos tell it, the river ran red and sorrowful for many weeks.

How many Miskitos and Sumus, how many Nicaraguan *campesinos,* were massacred? No one knows. All we are sure of is that the massacre took place on March 4, 1934, following the assassination of General Augusto Sandino in Managua on the night of February 21. The National Guard descended on the cooperative at Wiwilí, organized by Sandino and his followers to work for peace after they succeeded in forcing the U.S. Marines to leave the country. The Guard demolished the cooperative and massacred its inhabitants. All that remains is the Amerindians' memory of that river of blood, that current of death. The trauma in the Miskito community could not be erased.

Borge with Bishop Sergio Méndez Arceo of Cuernavaca, Mexico

There's an ideological, political, and moral parallel between those who massacred the Miskitos and Sumus back then, and those who kidnap and murder them today, trying to make them lose the path of their history, confusing them so that they will not encounter Sandinism, which would mean to find again their own lands and their river—a homeland at long last secured.

A PROFOUNDLY DEMOCRATIC PROCESS

The light of the Nicaraguan revolution is running the length and breadth of the Americas, reflecting off the skins of Quechuas, Aymaras, Guaranís, Zotzils; of whites, blacks, reds, copper-tones, mestizos; of all those who are exploited and discriminated against, and who see in this revolution the possibility of a world at last free of sorrow. And since the announcement in late 1984 of a process of autonomy for indigenous peoples and communities of the Atlantic Coast, our revolution has become even more noteworthy and controversial. . . .

What are the principles and objectives of this autonomy process? What are its implications both inside and outside the Atlantic Coast area and Nicaragua?

We have found no useful guidance in the history of Latin America, characterized as it is by horror and sadness; and there is little to be gleaned from other historical experiences. So we had to set out on this strategic journey with our own lantern and construction materials. It is an original, unique process that continues to point out contradictions and overcome obstacles with the agility of a young deer, in a dramatic race against time and hatred.

The first miracle for the inhabitants of the Atlantic Coast has been their transformation from objects to subjects of history. From the depths of their communities, they have brought forth a creation—autonomy—that is profoundly democratic. A great many leaders—men and women from throughout the country, and particularly from the Atlantic Coast—took part in a discussion that gave rise to the initial document entitled "Principles and Policies for the Exercise of the Rights of Autonomy by the Indigenous Peoples and Communities of the Atlantic Coast of Nicaragua." Dozens of these natural leaders then made valuable contributions to the national and regional autonomy commissions. There ensued hundreds of meetings, heated discussions, and agreements that opened the floodgates of an enormous popular consultation—a consultation that was a boiling pot of hopes, doubts, suspicions, optimism, and guilt complexes; an exchange that has been leading to greater trust, not only because of the justice of what is being proposed, but because of the likelihood of its realization.

The autonomy process, *compañeros,* has been born among the living and resurrected among the dead. It has proceeded in spite of staggering material limitations, relying on the participation of coastal communities whose elders and youths, women and men, have been the principal protagonists of this historical achievement. They formed an army of volunteers, unlearned in anthropological techniques, who improvised rustic but effective means of social mediation. Hundreds of these facilitators crisscrossed through the dust and mud of dirt roads, visiting communities and workplaces, going from house to house by sunlight and by moonlight, discussing the "Platform of Principles," learning what the inhabitants thought about autonomy.

This process of consultation gathered the views of churches, labor unions, government agencies, and even sectors of the armed opposition who agreed to a cease-fire. The consultation extended beyond questions and answers to a rich debate whose synthesis— autonomy—is today in the process of being fulfilled—irreversibly. The fundamental principles that informed the consultation and stimulated discussion were not pulled out of a hat; they were pulled out of the very life of the communities, and the communities were enriched in the process.

A NICARAGUAN TRINITY

The most fundamental principle—a sort of trinity—has to do with the relationship between the process of autonomy, the Sandinista revolution, and the irreversible existence of the [Nicaraguan] nation. Without revolution there can be no autonomy, no national unity—and what's more, no nation, no reverence for our immortal dead, no sovereignty, no dignity, nothing. The Sandinista revolution was undertaken to ransom our homeland, held hostage by foreign domination and domestic irrationality. Nicaragua never existed as a nation prior to July 19, 1979, except inchoately in the struggles of the masses throughout our history. Now that we have carried out a revolution to ransom our homeland, now that we have a nation with which to repair our past and recover our future—with which to discover and assume our own identity as Nicaraguans—we Nicaraguans are setting forth the autonomy process for the Atlantic Coast area, with the ambitious hope of having it become an archetype for the rest of the world.

It is with this in mind that the revolution set in motion this profoundly original process, which bears not the slightest resemblance to any project of the displaced oligarchy of Nicaragua or of the someday-to-be-displaced oligarchies of other Third World countries, oligarchies that have nothing national about them, unless you can see something national in the wagging tails of lap dogs.

The liberal and conservative oligarchies of Nicaragua surrendered the Atlantic Coast to the greed of foreign companies in exchange for devalued currency, just as they surrendered the entire country to the imperialists for a few dollars more.[1] These foreign companies proceeded to deplete our mineral reserves and devastate our forests. I won't even refer to what we received in exchange, because a single human being is more valuable to us than all the gold in Rosita and Bonanza.[2] Silicosis, to cite but one factor, has helped fill the cemeteries of the Atlantic Coast.

Only the revolution can create the conditions necessary to break the vicious circle of desolation and provide room for all ethnic expressions, within a society that guarantees equal development to the various cultures and their languages; a society that does away with ethnocentric vices and all the stupid and inhumane forms of racial discrimination that lead to notions of superiority of one group over another. With the tenacity of our shared ethnic and linguistic roots we intend to create a rainbow of inviolate and unified hues to bequeath to future generations.

REGIONAL AUTONOMY AND NATIONAL SELF-DETERMINATION

To the inhabitants of the Atlantic Coast, autonomy is more than just a response to their ethnic and cultural-linguistic aspirations. It includes the establishment of regional forms of government, with political and administrative structures that—within the context of the Nicaraguan nation—design and implement policies from the standpoint of regional realities.[3]

Autonomy also means developing the economic potential of the Atlantic Coast. Though autonomy includes respect for the past, it also suggests and demands changes and transformations. It is not a crystallized, petrified condition condemning our people to catalepsy and perpetual backwardness. As soon as we are able to resolve the contradiction between needs and possibilities, autonomy will mean social and economic progress, development of communities, schools, hospitals, universities and polytechnic institutes, paved roads and streets, deep-water ports, fisheries, the sustained-yield harvesting of precious woods, the rebirth of mining centers, the harnessing of rivers to produce electricity, the feel of sand beneath bare feet on blue-water beaches, a proliferation of rivers of milk and honey.

These are our dreams, Sandinista dreams. Have we no right to dream? We dream of selflessness and community-mindedness; have we no right to dream? We dream of defeating imperialism; have we no right to dream? I believe we have not only the right but the duty to dream, so long as we keep our feet firmly planted on the ground and our index fingers on our rifle triggers. The dream of autonomy, *compañeros,* comes closer to realization with each passing day. The roosters are already crowing. The sun, brothers and sisters of the coast, is about to rise.

Our view of autonomy rescues the past to project it into the future. The kingdom of Moskitia, created by the British colonial power, was not, properly speaking, a manifestation of autonomy.[4] Nor was the abandonment and demagogy implicit in enclave existence and *somocismo.*[5] We have in mind an integral autonomy, establishing the objective conditions for the exercise of rights in the areas of culture, economics, and politics; a revolutionary autonomy that uncompromisingly demands a radical change in society, eliminating factors that sustain discrimination and plunder. Autonomy, in the consensus that has emerged from popular consultation, demands the establishment of autonomous regions within the context of the unity and indivisibility of the Nicaraguan people and its territory, a unity that transcends ethnic-cultural diversities.

The autonomy process reaffirms the sovereignty and self-determination of our people, and expresses the intransigent intent of the Nicaraguan nation to adopt the political forms that best correspond to its national and historical interests. As President

Daniel Ortega emphasized on another occasion, regional autonomy does not hinder national unity; it consolidates it.

Autonomy is an essential component of the revolution that we will defend implacably and impeccably, serenely and unyieldingly, in the face of the weapons, lies, and millions of death dollars that seek to destroy not only the autonomy process but Nicaragua and its revolution as well. And because this revolution and this process of autonomy is defended not only by Nicaraguans but by persons and peoples from around the world, we invite you, dear guests, to join us in discussing the summary prepared by the Autonomy Commission of South Zelaya. The *compañeros* of North Zelaya are at work on their own document, which will surely have both similarities and dissimilarities with that of South Zelaya, demonstrating the profoundly democratic content of this process. It will then be up to a joint commission to present a final proposal to the National Constituent Assembly.

CONTRADICTIONS AND CONFLICTS

Some persons, sometimes out of ignorance of our history and sometimes out of ill will, either believe or would have others believe that all our ethnic problems are recent, having mysteriously appeared on the morning of July 19, 1979. The truth is that the roots of the many problems of our Atlantic Coast are much older than Ronald Reagan, dating back to the infamous days of colonialism, of governments that sold their birthright, of dictatorships that knew nothing of compassion.

With the coming of the Sandinista revolution, the region experienced a tremendous liberation of social forces, of creative will, of previously inhibited demands for the recognition of their rights as individuals and as communities. Such an expansion of sociocultural vitality inevitably led to the emergence of contradictions. As we have honestly admitted, there was a time when we were not prepared to understand this historical rebirth, with the result that these contradictions intensified. The historical enemy of the Nicaraguan people and of humanity, lurking wild beast that it is, has been taking advantage of these contradictions to foment conflict.

The most crucial contradictions are those between peace efforts and military campaigns. In this context one must include the accumulation and dissipation of forgetfulness and spite, the intercession of those bolts of lightning that illuminate and extinguish consciences, the balance between cultural encounters and misunderstandings, between fatigue and enthusiasm, . . . and the mystique of Sandinista cadres, archetypes of selflessness and risk-taking, and of the persistent interest of the FSLN in resolving this painful tragedy. The solution to these contradictions is not a matter of mathematical logic, nor is it simply anthropological. There can be no doubt that it is essentially political.

The imperialists have military strategists to direct their criminal hordes, to use the computers of death to calculate the number of casualties that would result from a military intervention. They also have some businesspersons and certain priests to lead their ideological task forces, and sociologists and anthropologists to search for weaknesses in our social constitution. The Atlantic Coast has been given special priority in the U.S. strategy of counterrevolution, and we suspect there are serious contingency plans for this important region. Part of the U.S. strategy consists in organizing and arming Miskito military units in support of the counterrevolution. The U.S. Congress specifically authorized $5 million for the counterrevolution in the region of the Atlantic Coast. To this must be added the portion of the millions of dollars authorized for the FDN[6] that are destined for the Atlantic Coast, together with a good part of the funds directly administered by the U.S. Central Intelligence Agency for its "covert operations."

THE SWORD POINTED AT THE ATLANTIC COAST

All this is directed against peace, against the process of autonomy. But even more serious are the U.S. preparations in Honduran territory, especially on the Atlantic Coast of Honduras, creating a military machine aimed at the heart of the Atlantic Coast of Nicaragua. There is a chronology to these preparations:

• In 1983, some 40,000 U.S. troops engaged in joint maneuvers—designated Ahuas Tara I—with 4,000 Honduran troops only 40 kilometers from our border. The exercises included practice landings on beaches similar to those of the Nicaraguan Atlantic Coast.

- Between August 1983 and February 1984, some 11,500 U.S. and Honduran troops took part in the Ahuas Tara II exercises, part of which included a massive amphibious landing near our border, ás two aircraft carriers in full combat readiness stood by. Four military bases were also constructed.
- The greatest amphibious landing in Central American history occurred in the course of the Universal Trek 85 maneuvers, with the participation of 36 warships and 11,000 U.S. troops.
- The U.S. armed forces built an air base at La Ceiba, on the Honduran Atlantic Coast, designed for rapid deployment operations.
- The runway of the Trujillo airport, in the Honduran department of Colón, was lengthened to accommodate U.S. C-130 transports.
- In Puerto Lempira, department of Gracias a Dios, another runway was built with the capacity to receive heavy U.S. transport aircraft.
- In the last few months the runway at Ursuna has been upgraded, as have the installations at Mokorón, permitting an increase in the number of rapid *piraña* assault launches available to the counterrevolution.

Our intelligence sources inform us that in the last few weeks the rate of supply of provisions and ammunition to the counterrevolutionaries has accelerated. Training camps have been rebuilt, with photographs of them appearing in the media. All this objectively improves their possibilities for launching aggression. It is probable that in the coming weeks and months they will launch increased acts of provocation along the Coco River from their bases on Honduran territory, with the intention of creating border incidents that would facilitate the intervention of the Honduran army and U.S. troops. . . .

No one can assess the price the Nicaraguan people would have to pay as a result of direct intervention by the U.S.A. . . . The invading soldiers would likewise pay an unforeseeable price, despite their experience and sophisticated weaponry. No thermometer can take the temperature of a people in combat readiness. No one can assess the price that would have to be paid by the peoples of Latin America, just as the directors of such a crime cannot predict the indignant and violent response of the peoples of Latin America. U.S. leaders underestimate the formidable strength of our people and the unbounded capacity for response of other peoples whose horizons they dare to obstruct.

A U.S. GOVERNMENT DISCOVERY: AMERINDIANS ARE HUMAN

The leaders of the U.S.A. try to artificially alter reality, which they view through faulty mirrors. They reverse the hierarchy of values, viewing human beings with contempt, and therefore instrumentalizing them. Hence no one was fooled when the U.S. administration suddenly noticed that Miskitos are human beings. In the past, still retained in the collective memory of the [Nicaraguan] nation, Miskitos and blacks were thought of only as cheap labor for lumbering and gold mining operations. They were insignificant creatures, subject to only obscure and marginal references in historical chronicles and academic treatises. Yet all of a sudden Buffalo Bill, that genocidal murderer of North American native peoples, speaking from his White House office decorated with redskin scalps, discovers that Miskitos are human beings, and that they are now victims of Sandinista genocide. From that moment on, enormous amounts of resources are dedicated to organizing the Miskitos into a counterrevolutionary army. They are supplied with weapons and misinformation as part of an operation code-named "Red Christmas," intended to split off part of the Nicaraguan territory and divide the Nicaraguan people.

When the leaders of the U.S.A. discovered that Miskitos were human beings, [Secretary of State] Alexander Haig presented members of the U.S. Congress with a photograph of Miskitos allegedly massacred by our army. The photograph was then given prominence in *Le Figaro,* in France. Later a small news item buried deep in the newspaper acknowledged that the photograph was of bodies mutilated by Somoza's National Guard. Despite how ridiculous this made Mr. Haig look, there was from him no word of self-criticism or even a sheepish smile.

About the same time [U.S. ambassador to the United Nations] Jeane Kirkpatrick announced that two hundred fifty thousand Miskitos were being held in concentration camps in Nicaragua.

Milady failed to first check into the facts: this number is almost four times the total Miskito population of Nicaragua. It is said that in this instance Madam Kirkpatrick held her breath, producing the appearance of a smile, for which she was rewarded when a *contra* task force was named after her.

Then Ronald Reagan, adopting a studied paternal pose at a dinner party organized to raise funds for the murder of Nicaraguans, presented to his audience—and to the television cameras—a sweet Miskito girl said to be a survivor of Sandinista genocide. The girl then candidly admitted she'd been born in the U.S.A. of Nicaraguan parents, and was not a Miskito.

With remarkable audacity Mr. Reagan accuses us of being narcotics traffickers, of having Angolan troops on the Atlantic Coast, of burning a Jewish synagogue, of posing a danger to the security of the U.S.A, of threatening Brazil, Patagonia, the North Pole, the Third World, the Basilica of St. Peter, democracy, the Statue of Liberty, and public morals. It is to be supposed that Mr. Reagan will soon accuse us of also being responsible for AIDS [acquired immune deficiency syndrome] and the decline of the U.S. dollar.

TRUTHS AND HALF-TRUTHS

None of these persons has the slightest intention of honoring the truth. The best they can do is make shameless use of half-truths.

The only truth in all this is that they have dedicated $100 million to the counterrevolution, and that among the beneficiaries of these resources are KISAN for death and the warmongering sector of MISURASATA.[7]

The only truth in all this is blood, tears, women and children turned into mincemeat, tens of thousands of adolescents in combat units exposed to risk and death, the anguish of mothers and fathers, brothers and sisters, spouses and children; and the truth that the U.S. Congress has made itself an accomplice to President Reagan's Central America policy.

The only truth in all this is the economic blockade and resultant shortages of basic items of consumption. This encourages speculation and cornered markets, which in turn distort prices. There is also the truth that almost half our resources are earmarked for a war that has been imposed upon us.

The only truth in all this is that Mr. Reagan's representatives, some of them invested with the symbols of Christianity, challenge our laws—believing themselves immune—and international law as well, in addition to assailing our sense of honor and authority.[8]

The only truth in all this is the profound contempt of the U.S. leadership for ethnic minorities, including their own. There is nothing accidental about U.S. law number 93–531, that partitions the [Hopi-Navajo joint use] area known as Big Mountain, separating Navajos from Hopis with a chain-link fence. What possible interest could be served by removing Navajos from land they have lived on for four hundred years? Peabody Coal Company, whose principal stockholder is the Bechtel Corporation—in which both Secretary of Defense Caspar Weinberger and Secretary of State George Schultz served as officers before entering government—is interested in exploiting those mineral-rich lands, without any concern for the fate of the Amerindians who were born there. They have yet to discover, just as Mr. Reagan, Mr. Schultz, and Ms. Kirkpatrick have, that Amerindians are human beings. . . .

OVERCOMING OUR MISTAKES

The mistakes we have made do not justify the mass murder of the Nicaraguan people, or condone the international outlawry of the president of the U.S.A. No one can deny us the right and the duty of self-defense, and we will continue to defend ourselves with the force of law and—within the context of revolutionary legality—with the law of force.

As you who are familiar with the issue are well aware, it is not the first time that the U.S. government—which pretends to have resolved its own ethnic problems (through genocide and contempt)—has sought to create or promote ethnic conflicts elsewhere with the aim of crushing popular liberation movements or of destabilizing democratic governments. It has done so in Asia [Indochina], in Africa [Angola], in the Middle East [Lebanon], and elsewhere, and will continue to do so for as long as it is the richest government in the world in terms of hatred and death.[9]

When we [Sandinistas] first went to the Atlantic Coast after the revolutionary triumph of July 19, 1979, we didn't even know the rudiments of the ethnic problem. Our cadres and functionaries on the Atlantic Coast knew nothing of anthropology. We arrived on the coast smiling but a little bit lost, friendly but mechanistic in our thinking. Though we never gave up our good will, we immediately began to elaborate vicious circles. It was not until recently that we regained a sense of reality and common sense.

We have publicly acknowledged our mistakes, seeking to learn from them in order to overcome them. No one can say we have acted in bad faith. The imperialists, on the other hand, have stirred up conflicts wherever possible with the deliberate intent of provoking an ethnic war that would tear our country apart.

We revolutionaries do not resign ourselves to bewailing reality; we are not fatalists. We will not adopt the cynicism of Latin American oligarchies that every now and then deplore the degraded condition of the ethnic groups in their countries, while maintaining their forces of oppression in full combat readiness against thirty million Amerindians. They will not move a finger or pass a law that is not intended to keep this immense population nailed to its cross—a sacrifice that in no way serves to atone for the abominable sin of the dominant classes, which will one day receive the punishment of hell: their discontinuance as dominant classes.

We have accepted the historical challenge of our multiethnic and multilingual inheritance, walking with the inhabitants of our Atlantic Coast on a new path that is being built even as it is being traveled. The ideologues of imperialism will not forgive us our audacity, as they alternate between rage and astonishment. They will never understand that our creative imagination is part of our revolutionary program.

IMPERIALISM AND AUTONOMY

Our form of response to the ethnic problem in Nicaragua has awakened interest throughout Latin America. That is no accident, given the multiethnic composition of our peoples, the similarity of conditions, and the fact that our revolution has opened possibilities of creative response. There can be no doubt that our response is worrisome to oligarchs and imperialists. Because autonomy means rights, land, breaking with the infernal logic of enclaves, depriving landlords and transnational corporations of their accustomed privileges, and above all setting an example for millions upon millions of Latin Americans who suffer discrimination because of their ethnic identity.

Imperialism will find ways to respond to some of the problems of Latin America. Someday, in a moment of brilliance, its survival instinct will lead it to deal constructively with the revolt of debtor states and to get rid of [Chilean dictator Augusto] Pinochet and [Paraguayan dictator Alfredo] Stroessner, massacrers of Mapuches and Guaranís. These adjustments will permit it to maintain Latin American dependency.

But it will never be able to resolve the ethnic problem. For imperialism to support autonomy would be like placing a pistol to its head and pulling the trigger, because it would go against its very essence.

What most confounds our enemies is that we Nicaraguans have announced the goal of unity amid diversity in the midst of aggression. They similarly failed to understand how we could hold elections in the middle of a war, just as they've been unable to understand our effusive poetry, and the beautiful and provocative agility of the dance around the maypole.[10]

The revolution will not hold back the hands of its historical clock on either the Pacific or the Atlantic, in either the north or the south, nor in the rivers, lakes, and surrounding seas, nor in the conscience of our revolutionary people.

Six days from now we will celebrate the seventh anniversary of the revolution, in Estelí. Throughout these seven long chapters in our history, we have ground all intentions of retreat and surrender into dust. We Nicaraguans, brothers and sisters to the peoples of all latitudes, offer the contribution of our sacrifices to humankind.

UNITED IN OUR DIVERSITY

In the years to come we will be united in our diversity, whether speaking Spanish, Miskito, Sumu, or English, whether our skins be white, black, maize-colored, or earth-colored, whether we be extroverted or introverted whether our eyes be watering with sweet and sad melodies or our hips and feet be swaying to a sensual rhythm. Whether we inhabit the rivers and forests of the Caribbean slope, or the fertile fields and bustling cities of the Pacific slope, we are all adventurers in the best sense of the word, warriors who are mortal enemies of war.

Nicaraguans, this crazy people—crazy because we have defied the golden calf—of heroes and saints, of mestizos, Miskitos, blacks, Sumus, Ramas, Caribs, will be integrated into a single national consciousness, a single process of liberation, in the homeland we have resurrected with our blood and resurrected so that it be immortal.

We have learned by heart our obligation to be loyal to the hopes of the peoples of the world, to the trust of the poor, to all the ethnic groupings that, from the vantage point of their calvary, are seeing the possibility of their liberation.

Someday all peoples will be free, as we Nicaraguans are free. Someday they will begin constructing a new society, as we Nicaraguans are doing. Someday they will be able to say as we do, "a free homeland or death!" Someday.

NOTES

1. While Nicaragua was under U.S. Marine occupation in 1913, the U.S. government negotiated the Bryan-Chamorro treaty with the Conservative puppet regime it had installed. The treaty granted the U.S. exclusive rights to build an interoceanic canal across Nicaragua, together with naval bases on the Caribbean (Corn Islands) and Pacific (Gulf of Fonseca) sides of the country. In return Nicaragua received a one-time payment of $3 million, most of which never left the U.S., as it was used to pay off debts owed to U.S. banks by Nicaragua. The loans in question had in turn been imposed on Nicaragua as part of what was termed "dollar diplomacy," a policy designed to subordinate Central American and Caribbean countries to the U.S.A. through financial dependency. Though the money was ostensibly loaned to reform the Nicaraguan currency system, it was for the most part used to pay off Conservative collaborators in the U.S.-led overthrow of the more nationalist Zelaya/Madriz government. Both the Conservative governments of Díaz and Chamorro in the early part of the century and the Liberal governments of the Somozas in the middle part of the century sold land and mineral concessions on Nicaragua's Caribbean slope to U.S. companies at giveaway prices. For an excellent analysis, see Karl Bermann, *Under the Big Stick: Nicaragua and the U.S. Since 1848* (Boston: South End Press, 1986).

2. Rosita and Bonanza are gold mines located in the Siuna region of northeastern Nicaragua. Borge's point is an extension of the one made by Sandino in 1928 when he seized and destroyed the U.S.-owned mines of La Luz and Los Angeles.

3. The autonomy process as currently envisioned is to lead to the establishment of two autonomous regions: one encompassing the Miskitos and Sumus in northeastern Nicaragua (North Zelaya), the other encompassing the blacks, Caribs, and Ramas in the south-central coastal region (South Zelaya) surrounding Bluefields. Each region is to have its own assembly consisting of representatives freely elected by local communities. These assemblies will be responsible for regional legislation, for selecting regional administrators, and for safeguarding ethnic and linguistic rights.

4. When the British first arrived on Nicaragua's Caribbean coast in the 1560s, they encountered the Miskitos, who then dwelt only in a narrow fringe along the seacoast. After successfully incorporating the Miskitos into their raids on Spanish shipping, the British began trading guns for sea turtles. The Miskitos then used their formidable technological advantage to conquer the Sumus, until then the dominant Amerindian population of the region. As their Miskito proxies achieved hegemony, the British imposed a local monarch on them in 1687 to circumvent their traditional councils of elders and exercise effective control over the region. For further detail, see Bernard Nietschmann, *Between Land and Water: The Subsistence Ecology of the Miskito Indians, Eastern Nicaragua* (New York: Seminar Press, 1973), ch. 3.

5. The enclave system Borge speaks of is that of U.S. corporations that came to extract gold, silver, and valuable tropical woods. These were boom-and-bust operations that provided temporary employment and company stores, but took no care of the land and of the health of employees in their rush to extract profits. When they left as suddenly as they came, the regional economy stagnated.

6. *Fuerza Democrática Nicaragüense,* Nicaraguan Democratic Force, the official title of the principal *contra* organization, headquartered in Miami, Florida. Its political director is Adolfo Calero; its military director is Enrique Bermúdez, a former colonel in Somoza's National Guard (see also note 8, below, and ch. 14, note 4, above). If Ronald Reagan were to have his way, and if history were to repeat itself à la Somoza, Bermúdez would be installed as military chief of Nicaragua, and would eventually assume dictatorial power.

7. Miskito political divisions are reflected in the multiplication of organizations that have sprung up among them. When the Sandinistas first came to power in 1979, they promoted the formation of MISURASATA (a Miskito acronym for "Miskito, Sumu, Rama, and Sandinista together").

Its leader, Steadman Fagoth, broke off in 1981 to form the counterrevolutionary guerrilla organization MISURA, based in Honduras. His successor, Brooklyn Rivera, then departed for Costa Rica, from which he organized a rival guerrilla organization under the name MISURASATA (MISURASATA leader Hazel Lau remained in Nicaragua, where she has since been elected as an FSLN delegate to the National Assembly). Segments of MISURASATA and MISURA regrouped as KISAN in 1985 in order to receive U.S. financing. All these organizations have since split into "peace" and "war" factions, mirroring opposing pressures from Amerindian communities and CIA paymasters.

8. The reference is in large measure to Bishop Pablo Antonio Vega of Juigalpa, who on July 2, 1986 denounced the previous week's decision of the World Court in the case of *Nicaragua vs. U.S.A.* as "partial." In a 12 to 3 decision, the International Court of Justice based in The Hague, Netherlands, had found "that the United States of America, by training, arming, equipping, financing, and supplying the contra forces . . . against Nicaragua, has acted . . . in breach of its obligation under customary international law not to intervene in the affairs of another state," "that the U.S.A. is under a duty immediately to cease and to refrain from all such acts . . . ," and "that the U.S.A. is under an obligation to make reparation to the Republic of Nicaragua for all injury caused" ("Excerpts from Ruling by the World Court," *New York Times*, June 28, 1986, p. 4).

9. The CIA organized highland tribes of Vietnam and Laos to combat communist forces in the Indochinese war of the 1960s and 1970s, with the result that these peoples were decimated. For a while in the 1980s, the Reagan administration backed the Maronite Christian Phalangists in factional warfare in Lebanon, and is now backing the tribally-based UNITA forces in Angola against the country's Marxist government.

10. The Maypole, *palo de mayo,* is the traditional May Day celebration of the black Creole communities of the Caribbean coast. Unlike maypole celebrations elsewhere, this one centers on rhythmic, sensual dancing to African-inspired Caribbean music.